THE SPIRIT OF
BOB HOPE
★ *One Hundred Years* ★ *One Million Laughs* ★

Website: richardgrudens.com

THE SPIRIT OF
BOB HOPE

★ *One Hundred Years* ★ *One Million Laughs* ★

by
RICHARD GRUDENS

Author of
The Best Damn Trumpet Player
The Song Stars
The Music men
Jukebox Saturday Night
Snootie Little Cutie
Jerry Vale-A Singer's Life
Magic Moments

CELEBRITY PROFILES PUBLISHING
Box 344 Main Street
Stony Brook, New York 11790-0344
(631) 862-8555

Published by
Celebrity Profiles Publishing Company
Div. Edison & Kellogg
Box 344 Main Street
Stony Brook, New York 11790-0344
(631) 862-8555
Fax (631) 862-0139
Email: celebpro4@aol.com

Library of Congress Control Number: 2001096778
ISBN: 1-57579-227-3

Printed in the United States of America
PINE HILL PRESS, INC.
Sioux Falls, SD 57106

TABLE OF CONTENTS

A PRAYER

"We pray that "The Spirit of Bob Hope"
will be a success and that many people will enjoy
learning more about this wonderful entertainer.
May God bless you."

Evangelist Billy Graham
August, 2001

Bob and Billy Graham
(courtesy NBC)

INTRODUCTION
BY RICHARD GRUDENS

You may ask, who is Bob Hope? Almost everyone from the age of ten to ninety knows the answer to that question. And Bob Hope knows just about everyone. He has entertained tens of millions live and otherwise his entire life. When you meet him, you think you know him, and you do!

On May 29, 2003, Bob will celebrate his 100th birthday, most of those years in front of an audience. This book is a tribute dedicated to that most significant day.

Since 1952 I have been a Bob Hope chronicler. As an NBC guest relations representative, and later, Broadcast Ticket Division manager attending to seating arrangements for radio and television shows during the

....

Our first meeting 1984, Westbury N.Y. *(C. Camille Smith photo)*

....

1950s, I worked some of Bob's live TV specials and radio programs including *The Big Show*, where Bob appeared as one of Tallulah Bankhead's guests on radio's last—ditch offense against the invasion of television, and actually the last really big- time radio show; on the *Colgate Comedy Hour* when originating in New York, and during other radio and television productions. Since those days, I have contributed a number of articles to entertainment and traditional magazines describing Bob's career drawn from personal interviews with Bob and those who know him best.

In September, 1993, World War II Magazine commissioned my extensive interview conducted with Bob in 1984, documenting his ubiquitous wartime travels with his marvelous troupe of USO performers. It was transformed into a feature article, earning a full cover treatment. Bob has always been gracious, caring, funny and charming during interviews whether in person backstage at Long Island's Westbury Music Fair (his then annual treat for Long Islanders); in his suite at the nearby Garden City Hotel, or the East Norwich Inn (owned then by composer Burt Bacharach) or simply over the phone from his Hope Enterprises, Burbank, California office, or wherever you could reach him; and you usually could.

In 1998 Bob Hope composed a foreword for *The Music Men*, my book describing the careers of the popular male singers from Al Jolson and Bing Crosby to Frankie Laine and Jerry Vale, whose careers proliferated throughout the 1920s through the 1960s. Bob's contribution, entitled *Those Wonderful Guys*, was managed gratefully by Ward Grant, Bob's longtime press agent, assisting busy Bob and I in working it out.

So, how do you begin writing a book about Bob Hope, perhaps the most well known personality in the world? There have been many other books, you know, written by Bob himself and other authors, authorized and unauthorized, punctuating notable milestones in his wondrous life.

Well, you start with his uneventful birth in London, England, and early childhood in nearby Eltham, just this side of the turn-of-the-century, and subsequent youthful emigration to America. You document his fledgling singing and dancing experiences on vaudeville stages all over America where he honed those remarkable, comedic skills that would serve him so well later on in a number of Broadway shows, on the long-running Pepsodent radio show, performing in those Paramount Studios Crosby, Hope and Lamour *Road* movies, on endless TV appearances, and performing in those major USO military entertainment tours beginning with World War II, weaving his way through Korea, Vietnam, and Desert Storm.

So here goes: *The Spirit of Bob Hope.* One Hundred Years-One Million Laughs.

Richard Grudens
Stonybrook, New York
August 2001

(But, first, some noteworthy words from his friend and mine, the beautiful "Buttons & Bows" girl, Jane Russell, who, by the way, personally submitted the photo appearing in her foreword.)

FOREWORD

BY JANE RUSSELL

Nobody needs to tell you that Bob Hope is a one-of-a-kind personality, and a Gemini. I don't know if he has so many lifelong friends and helpers because he's so relaxed and amusing—or if he's relaxed and amusing 99 percent of the time because he has an army of old loving friends and family who would do anything for him, anything in the world.

I've been lucky enough to be around him making two pictures, *Paleface* and *Son of Paleface*, and on many trips through the states on military bases and aircraft carriers during the war to entertain the troops, and I have never seen this darling man upset or losing his cool in any situation. In part of his comedy in film he plays a guy getting utterly rattled or scared—but, believe me, that's only in the movies—not for one second after the director has called cut. Working with him has been nothing but fun. His name for me was "Lumps."

Jane and "Bob and those fat lips and Big Brown Eyes." *(Jane Russell collection)*

One day it was about 4:45 and we'd finished a shot and the next one was a large scene, which was going to need more lighting, and Bob looked at his watch and then casually announced, 'Well, this looks like it's going to take awhile, and I think I could get in about nine holes before dark, so I'll see you all tomorrow.' And he sauntered across the stage and out the door as we all stood slack-jawed, staring after him. As the stage door closed, director Norman McCloud, a darling man with his own sense of humor, stomped his foot and whined, "Bob, you come back here!" We all roared with laughing and went home. Only the crew stayed to light the set for the first shot tomorrow.

He is totally Mr. Relaxed, with a marvelous sense of humor. The only thing that never rests are those chocolate brown eyes, which never miss a thing going on in any room he's in—while awake.

Oh, and that reminds me—In New York at the Paramount Theater he could drop off to sleep between the six shows a day for about fifteen minutes and wake up totally refreshed. I wanted to kill him. I had to struggle to get my nine hours in every night while wearing eye shades and earplugs so the 3 a.m. drunks in the hall wouldn't wake me up. I even got a hotel across the street so I didn't waste time in cabs, while he stayed across town on the chic side. One morning I overslept and came tearing across the street in my fur coat, and heard him about to introduce me. I rushed to the wings and opened my coat to show him my flannel nightgown. He just giggled and went on with another bevy of jokes till I got into the beaded gown in my dressing room and then threw on some lipstick.

Oh, I take that back. I did see him upset once. When he was due at a military or charity do, it was his habit to get to the show just a bit before he was to appear on stage, and when he was through, to walk very quickly out the door to the car where his buddies were waiting for him with the car running. He'd done it before the fans even knew what happened. But the rest of us got trapped in the mob for hours. So I announced to him that the next time I was going in his car with him. He looked very agitated and said, "Oh, no, you can't. You'll never get changed in time." The next time I walked just as fast right behind him and got in with my beaded dress and dangled earrings right beside him. I'm a Gemini too.

Years later, at a show in Palm Springs while I was onstage, people were asking questions about leading men and someone asked, of all my leading men—Mitchum, Gable, etc. etc., who was the best kisser? Without a second thought I said, "Bob Hope." It was wonderful kissing those big, soft, flabby lips. Mmmm yeah!!!

Coming onstage, Bob hollered, "I wasn't even trying."

So enjoy this book about our darling, one-of-kind Gemini cool cat. By the way, Dolores is a Gemini too."

Jane Russell

Montecito, California, July 2001

AFTERWORD

BY KATHRYN CROSBY

Throughout most of my adulthood, I viewed Bob Hope as a splendid adjunct to my life with Bing. But it was actually Bob whom I first met.

Here's how it happened: The year was 1954. For my newspaper column *Texas Girl* in Hollywood, I was interviewing Joan Fontaine and Bob on the set of "Casanova's Big Night."

Kathryn and Bing Crosby *(Kathryn Crosby collection)*

Unburdened by my 18 summers and total lack of preparation, I plunged straight into my version of investigative journalism.

Bob simply smiled, but his ripely beguiling costar took umbrage at queries such as, "How old were you when you made those wonderful films in the thirties, when you won your Oscar in 1941 for your role of Lina in "Suspicion? So how old does that make you now?"

Joan was preparing to stomp the obstreperous adolescent into oblivion with her four-inch heels, when Bob intervened with the following: "Making allowances for your youth and inexperience, we still can't let you talk to a great star that way. Now, here's what you should have asked:"

Then he proceeded to pose a series of pertinent questions, couched in highly laudatory terms, to which Joan vouchsafed amused answers which I hastily scribbled down.

It was a gentle and instructive rebuke from a master craftsman, and I never forgot the lesson that it instilled. Months later, when the same callow teen-ager interviewed

Bing for her paper, she was ready to snare a superstar and a husband with a far more subtle approach.

So, Bob Hope, fabulous teacher and friend, thanks again for everything.

Kathryn Crosby
Genda, Nevada
August 2001

★★★★★★★★★★★★★★★★★★★★★★★★★★★★★★★★★

ACT ONE:
THE CURTAIN RISES

LIFE IN CLEVELAND

At age 8 shooting for the moon
(courtesy Fredrick Muller-England)

VISIONS OF AMERICA

*"I left England when I found out
I could never be King."*

Born in London, England to a master stonemason father and a Welch mother who aspired to a concert singer's life in show business, Leslie Towns Hope began celebrating life on May 29, 1903 in the village of Eltham. There were four older brothers; Ivor, James, Fred, William (called Jack); a sister (Emily) who died before he was born; two younger brothers Sidney, and George (the only one born in the U.S.) and a life of moving from one village to another while his ever disillusioned, but otherwise optimistic Mother, Avis Towns whom all the boys called "Ma'am," inspired him to entertain the family at a very early age, especially when his father would sometimes cavort and drink excessively at local pubs when life proved too difficult for him at a given moment. He always told his boys that dust from the stone settled in his throat, so he stopped often at pubs after a days work. Young Leslie helped keep the otherwise bored family in brighter spirits.

"They said, when I was five, I would visit my Great Aunt Polly who was over 100. I would do impersonations of people we knew to make her laugh. 'Always leave 'em laughing, laddie, 'she would tell me and then hand me a cake or cookie like I was a little puppy doing a trick. Guess to her, I was."

Little Leslie's life was once saved by his oldest brother Ivor when Leslie swam out too far in Herne Bay at Canterbury, and almost drowned.

"I was a little show-off but I ran out of steam and almost didn't make it back. Ivor rescued me and someone worked me over and I began breathing again. In fact, that's how I got my ski-nose....doing show-off comedy. I once climbed an apple tree, and, being a clown, always looking for attention, reached up too high on a branch and lost my balance. My nose paid the price, not that anyone ever noticed—well, except Bing Crosby—I used to tell everyone that my mother would say they took her baby and left her the stork."

Bob has characterized that his *ski-nose*, popularized by a phrase coined by Crosby, was really a genetic feature, and that his brother Fred had the same anatomical quirk.

Leslie Hope possessed a youthful, happy heart and dispelled his mother's desperation delivering for her his early, distinctive brand of humor. His future career, performing comedy was apparent to the family even then, and present at a time when his mother needed "laughs" the most from her talented middle son.

Looking across the Atlantic for much needed employment in his trade, and encouraged by relatives who had crossed earlier, Leslie's father emigrated to Cleveland, Ohio, finding lucrative employment for awhile setting stone on area churches, schools, and public buildings. William Henry Hope's letters to the family back in England inspired Avis Hope, and though she worried about the insecurity of leaving England, unshakably decided to follow her husband's advice to pack up and sail to America with all the children in tow.

"I was only five, but my global travels had already begun. The voyage was rough, all of us berthing in noisy, hot steerage cabins, right above the main drive shaft of the ship, but in March of 1908 we passed through Ellis Island like a bunch of immigrants and headed to Cleveland, Ohio by train for a HOPEful *new and better life*, especially for our Ma'am."

However, life for the Hope family in Cleveland turned out to be not very different than living in England. Harry, as his father was known, had not changed his habits, and their modest quarters on Euclid Street in the bustling city of Cleveland was certainly no improvement over the row house they shared in England built by his grandfather James Hope, also a stonemason, who had participated in carving intricate parts for the construction of the Statue of Liberty in Paris. In fact, life in Cleveland was a bit worse, the family having to learn the dialect of a new country and needing to find new friends in a more frenzied atmosphere.

"HOPELESS" STRIKES BACK

In school, Les Hope was labeled "Hopeless, " but his fast fists and nimble feet put a quick end to that unwanted *sobriquet*.

"When kids asked me my name, I said 'Les Hope,' and wise guys translated that into *Hopeless*. As a result, *I* and *they* wound up with a bloody nose or two. My dad had trained us boys to fight—to protect ourselves in this new, *uncertain* land called Cleveland."

Unfortunately, his dad's trade was again in trouble, stone setting being less and less in demand for building than locally manufactured brick, and returned to his drinking indiscretions. His mother, stronger, steadier, and more focused on family concerns, tried to ignore her husband's philandering to concentrate on instilling strength and resolve into her boys, preparing them in her own way for the hard times she imagined lay ahead for them in the absence of a strong father, one who readily succumbed to negative outside interests during personal reversals. To be fair, however, Harry was always a "buddy" to his kids, encouraging them to help take care of their mother and to always work to earn money for themselves, even at an early age. There were times the children's' earnings were the only income the family had to pay for food and rent. Despite the financial setback, Avis moved the family into a larger house with an increased rent, but leased rooms to boarders to make up the difference.

"Ma'am worked hard and kept a clean, organized home. Every Saturday night we took a bath in a metal tub. The best kid of the week would go first. I never went first. I always thought water was gray until bottled water came out. Since then, when I walk into a luxury hotel and see those gleaming bathroom fixtures, I remember that galvanized job in the kitchen, soap in my eyes, and Ma'am dunking us."

His mother always met the family's obligations head-on, even if it meant trudging through snow and sleet to, for instance, pay the butcher on time. She kept the boys clean and clothed, even altering cast off clothing. Like many mothers of that time, her life was washing, ironing and cooking and little else.

To earn pocket cash for himself Leslie would either sing or shoot pool. Aboard a streetcar bound for nearby Luna Park with his brothers and friends, young Les would sing popular songs then pass the hat to earn admittance to the park, and for refreshments. Those earnings were his only pocket money.

"By the time I was seven or eight I had a pretty good voice. Halfway between high tenor and soprano. So on Sundays when we were broke, it seemed natural for a bunch of my brothers and I to hop a streetcar and sing for crowds headed to Luna Park. I'd give out with a solo, then we'd do a quartet. Then we'd beat it before the motorman threw us off."

Sometimes those few bucks were converted to family use. And, sometimes the money was spent at the neighborhood theater box office for Les and his brothers to watch their favorite movie stars on the silent screen. Les would always imagine himself as Rudolph Valentino or Charlie Chaplin. Chaplin was King. These larger than life celluloid figures were his inspiration—his mentors.

"My dad drank a little too much sometimes. He was a funny guy, too. When he didn't come home for dinner we would find him in a bar entertaining the other patrons. He had a wonderful sense of humor.

"Anyway, I was better off at the movies where I couldn't get into trouble. There were times I got in trouble and was even locked up once for burglarizing a sports store with some friends. We did it for the tennis equipment, not for money. It turned out Ma'am and Dad's punishment were far worse than any the cops dished out."

That was the beginning and end of Les Hope's crime spree. To make a buck in those days he did everything every other kid did—shined shoes, raked up leaves, soda jerked, caddied at the golf course, was a shoe clerk, worked in his brother Fred's meat market, and sold newspapers. He once had a regular customer, an old man who was driven around by a chauffeur in a brougham, tell him—when he bought a newspaper from Les one day on his corner—and didn't have change of a dime: "Go get change!" the stranger insisted.

"I told him I would trust him until the next day, but he objected, 'No! Go get change!' Sure, I lost a couple of paper sales, so when I got back from getting change at the candy store, he said, 'See, you lost business because you didn't have change. The way to run a business is to always be ready and always deal in cash and have ready change and don't give credit.' That was an expensive lesson, but I never forgot it. By the way, the man turned out to be John D. Rockefeller, Sr., the richest man in the world at the time. How about that!"

BATTERED BOXER

Bob, constantly driven, diligently tried everything to achieve success of one kind or another. He took up professional boxing. When in England, and later in Cleveland, his father instructed his sons in boxing. Bob practiced hard everyday and decided to enter the Ohio State amateurs as a lightweight. Sixteen and determined, he named himself Packy West, (there was a Packy East-Packy McFarland,) and considered it an impressive name for a fighter. As luck would have it, he creamed his first opponent and now possessed a false sense of security.

"What confidence! After another win, they placed me in the semi-finals. Then I learned I had to fight Happy Walsh. It was like saying, 'Tonight you fight King Kong'. When I stepped into the ring I became numb. Happy kept smiling. Fists, knives, or bullets never bothered him. He had muscles on his muscles. Everyone was smiling except me. I got out of the ring alive, however. They carried me out in the second round. That closed the door on my boxing career."

Ivor, Leslie (Bob), Jack and Jimmy Hope - circa 1910.
(Bob Hope Collection)

★★★★★★★★★★★★★★★★★★★★★★★★★★★★★★★

ACT TWO:
VAUDEVILLE CIRCUITS
GETTING READY FOR THE BIG TIME

Sharing stages with Mildred Rosequist
(circa 1920s, courtesy Fredrick Muller-England)

Getting Ready
for the Big Time

Charlie Chaplin's antics on screen had deeply penetrated Leslie Hope's psyche. Here, he rationalized, was a comedic genius who also hailed from London, near where the Hope family once lived, and became the King of Hollywood in different place called America, the same land where Les now lived. Mesmerized by the pantomime creations of Chaplin to the extent that Les would dress up in ragged shoes that flapped, an old suit, and a piece of rattan for a swinging cane, to pretend he was Chaplin, right down to the famous duck—legged walk, Hope performed at Luna Park in Cleveland, entering a contest emulating the comic genius, winning enough prize money to buy a cooking stove that he and his friends carried home to the delight of his mother. Les Hope was distinctly proud of his effort and was now totally struck with the idea of a career in show business.

"I thought, 'Hey, maybe me! Why not? I can do it. I want to do it.' Much later, I think it was 1927, I actually saw Chaplin for the first time in New York. I remember standing in the doorway of the Forty-Second Street Theater for a couple of hours just waiting to see him—to be in his illustrious company for only a moment. I was already an ambitious vaudeville headliner, nevertheless I remained a serious follower of the great comedian. I felt comfortable having finally met him face to face."

Les loved to sing and always sang around the house. His singing teacher's pet, music was his best subject. Avis was a fine singer of Welsh songs and would perform at the annual Cleveland Welsh Picnic. All the Hopes would participate singing those traditional Welsh songs together.

Few realize Les Hope spent many years in a somewhat sparkling career as a singer, dancer, and then comedian from 1929 through 1937 on endless vaudeville circuits from his start in Cleveland right up through his triumphant performances at vaudeville's *Carnegie Hall*, the famous Palace Theater on New York's Great White Way.

"Besides Chaplin's influence, it was Ma'am who took me to see comedian Frank Fay at Keith's vaudeville theater in

Cleveland. She knew about my theatrical ambitions. After Fay worked the audience with his opening monologue, Ma'am looked at me and said loudly, 'He's not as half as good as you,' and I said, 'S-h-h-h, Ma, please!'"

"'I don't care,' she insisted, 'He can't sing or dance as well as you.' Of course he could! She didn't wait long enough to find out. Many years later I played the same theater and Ma'am was there to see it. 'It's about time. They should have recognized your own genius sooner.' That's my Ma'am!"

For many years Hope struggled through a number of partnerships with dancers and comedians right up through his work as a star with the Ziegfeld Follies. This was well before Bob's involvement in radio, which finally established him nationally, elevating him into films. Les introduced some great songs that have become standards while appearing on Broadway and performing in films: "I Can't Get Started," his signature theme "Thanks for the Memory," "It's De-Lovely," "Smoke Gets In Your Eyes," "I Can't Get Started," "Two Sleepy People," "Buttons and Bows," "You Do Something to Me," and "Silver Bells." Everyone a standard evergreen today.

Dorothy Lamour said, "Bob always wanted to be a singer, but everybody pushed it aside. They said, 'No! You're a comedian, you're not a singer! But to me he was a singer and he still is a singer, and a very good singer, but the public would not accept him that way."

Les Hope accepted dancing lessons from an old-time vaudeville dancer, Johnny Root, who one day decided to relocate to California, leaving Les with the business, so Les had business cards printed that read:

Lester Hope
Will Teach You To Dance
Buck & Wing- Soft shoe; and Eccentric Waltz Clog

"My girlfriend at the time was Mildred Rosequist. She was fifteen. We worked up a dance act and played a few local dates. We'd split the 8 to 10 bucks. We would show the audience different steps saying 'We learned this dance in the parlor,' or 'We learned this dance in the kitchen,' and they loved it. The applause went to my head."

Les wanted to leave Cleveland with Mildred to search for work in the theater, mostly on the road, but her mother wouldn't have it. So he convinced Lloyd Durbin, a local kid he knew with similar aspirations, to join up with him. At one Cleveland theater date they met silent screen star, Fatty Arbuckle, who introduced them to the manager of the Bandbox, who was willing to hire them to perform a soft-shoe and sing tunes like "Sweet Georgia Brown." Their big number was a comedic Egyptian dance accomplished in pantomime while wearing bowler hats, pretending to dip the hat in the Nile River and bringing it back.

"The gag was that afterward we poured actual water out of the derby. It was real crazy and grabbed lots of laughs that kept us working for a while."

Thanks to Arbuckle, the boys linked up with a touring show called *The Jolly Follies*. From East Palestine, Ohio, to Ottawa, Ohio, the pair did their stuff. Audiences in those days were tough on new acts. They traveled by bus. Living conditions were also tough. And strange things would happen. Rolled curtains came down too often with a crash, scaring patrons. Actors fought among themselves on stage, especially family acts. Usually, the theaters had only two dressing rooms, one for guys and one for gals. If you were not an important enough act, you dressed in the basement coal bin, but first you had to clean it up and find a table on which you could store your clothes. You also learned to cook hash over a hot plate and wondered if you would eat again the next day.

Only quality vaudeville circuits, like Keith or Orpheum, assigned acts a private dressing room. In the twenties, touring vaudevillians earned forty to fifty dollars a week, which was not bad. Some acts spent ten years or more on these circuits creating a nice, steady living. The audience was tougher than a jury of madmen. Many actors had other day jobs.

"We were sitting on stage and asked the house manager what time the rehearsal began. He explained the rehearsal was at 5:30 because the fiddle player worked at the butcher shop and got off work at 5:15. All this mayhem was needed experience that prepared me for what was to come: Broadway."

For Les Hope, acquiring skills, like getting up in front of a theater full of people easily was the most natural thing in the world for him after working in the *Follies*.

Future headliners Jack Benny, Fred Allen, George Burns and Gracie Allen, Red Skelton, Milton Berle, Red Buttons, among other contemporaries, also earned their stripes on vaudeville circuits as did young Les and Lloyd. All were products of vaudeville's harsh proving grounds, preparing them for greater challenges to come—if only they could last long enough.

"Me and Lloyd lasted a year. Tragically, Lloyd ate some coconut pie and died as a result of food poisoning, but mostly because he couldn't get the medical attention he needed fast enough, although I think he was weakened by some other illness and didn't know it. He never looked very healthy. George Byrne became my new partner. He was a smooth dancer and had a nice personality. We became partners and friends."

The boys regularly introduced new comedy sketches into their act. Very ambitious, they also sang in the show's quartet and performed extra character parts in other acts, but they wanted to achieve even more.

"We tried black face, but after the first show we couldn't get the stuff off our faces until three in the morning. We had used black grease instead of burnt cork. How were we to know? We needed a blowtorch to get it off. Anyway, that was our first and last black face appearance."

After the show's run the boys circled back to Cleveland, directly to the Hope family home. They badly needed some R & R. The home cooked food was heaven to them. They practiced in front of the mirror over the fireplace and made the house shake with laughter. Les' mom would be their appreciative audience.

Sometimes, Les would hop in his Ford Model "T" and drive to nearby Morgantown to see his sweetheart, Mildred.

"Once, on the way to Mildred's, a swarm of bees invaded my Model "T" and penetrated my clothing. I acted crazy and drove like a madman right into a farmer's barn to escape the swarm. I speedily peeled off my clothes like a stripper at the Palace. At first the farmer thought I was a lunatic, but he

Vaudeville
Days with
George Byrne
and Bob Hope
*(Bob Hope
collection)*

finally helped me chase off the buggers. I was stung a dozen times. Oh, what I did for love."

Les and George continually polished up their comedy routines. George would walk across a stage with a suitcase, put it down, then stepped over it. Les would ask, "How are you?" George would answer, "Fine, just getting over the grippe." Then he'd walk across again with a woman's dress on a hanger, and Les would say, "Where are you going?" and he'd say, "Down to get this filled."

Or he'd walk across with a big wooden plank under his arm. Les would say, "Where are you going?" And he'd say, "To find a room, I've already got my board."

"And, how about the one where George looked down inside his pants and I'd ask, 'What are you doing?' and he'd say, 'The doctor told me to watch my stomach.' That's the kind of material we'd get away with in those days and that we thought was pretty good at the time.

"Or, I'd walk on and say, 'Pardon me, would you give me a dime for a cup of coffee?' And he'd say, 'A dime for a cup of coffee? **I'm an actor!**' And I said, 'You're an actor? and he said, 'Yes,' So I said, 'Come in and I'll buy *you* a cup.'"

In their two seasons with the *Follies*, besides singing and dancing, the comedy routines increased. Routines went like this:

"This fellow from out of town stopped at a hotel and asked the manager for a room and a *bath*. The manager said," I can give you a room." and the guy says, "I asked for a room and a bath!" So, the manager says, "I can give you a room, but you'll have to take the bath yourself."

In those days stuff like that always got laughs. No one now knows why.

Les and George worked the vaudeville circuits with all their compatriots who were searching for the same fame and fortune that eludes most performers over long careers. The boys tried everything they could to build up their act, always coming out battling, always trying and trying:

"*Vaudeville* and *headliners* are spelled with the same number of letters. But the team of Hope & Byrne lent little thought to the fact that *heartbreak*, too, used the same number. Before very long we were to find that out."

Hating his current state of anonymity, Les Hope burdened himself with need to be recognized. He needed to be noticed, and to be known. He wanted the world to know he was *Les Hope, the Great Vaudevillian.* He'd pull his car up at traffic stops and shout to anyone within hearing distance: "Have you folks been to the Orpheum this week to see Les Hope? You should! He's great!" He would proceed to tell everyone about the show. Then he would step on the gas and drive off, pleased with his wit and gift for gathering publicity, and headed to another stop to repeat his outdoor advertising act.

Remember, there was no radio, talking films, or television, only vaudeville or circuses existed for most folks entertainment.

Les felt he eventually had to go it alone...a single...but first a break was needed once again back in Cleveland with some of Ma'am's good cooking. He needed a fresh, new act. Singing, dancing, talking, and, maybe working in black face—maybe!

He ate and slept at home for a while and hopped the streetcar to the theater. He bought a big red bow tie and white cotton gloves like his hero, Al Jolson. He added a cigar and a small derby that jiggled up and down when he bounced onstage.

"I picked up a few things I'd worked up myself, and for an encore I did a song and dance. I scored well, even if I was scoring in a minor league. One night I arrived too late for applying makeup and black cork, and, my good luck held—I scored even better."

Les thought his profile quite handsome, and the more he reflected upon it the more he realized it was a good thing he had no time that night to makeup his face, although he didn't realize it's value at that moment.

(R. Grudens collection)

Once, while emceeing on a bill in New Castle, Pennsylvania, Bob introduced an act for a well-known vaudeville Scotsman: "Ladies and Gentlemen, next week Marshall Walker will be here. I know him. He got married in the back yard so the chickens could get the rice." Bob's standup career had started, the house roared. The theater manager loved it, and inadvertently discovered *Bob Hope*.

FROM LES TO BOB IN CHICAGO

After trying unsuccessfully to market his *single* act in Cleveland, Leslie Hope moved on once again to Chicago and there altered his name to *Lester*. Without employment, he rapidly ran out of funds, piling up local coffee and doughnut debt. Luck flowed his way when he ran into an old friend who introduced him to an agent, who promptly booked him into a spot at the Stratford Theater as an emcee, a role he was slowly developing. Wondrously, the two week gig lasted a full six months. Twenty five dollars a week became two hundred. He hustled comic material from other acts and magazines, and anywhere he could.

"Sometimes I'd tell a bad joke, make a face and blame it on my brother who I said—'writes them for me.' I'd say things like, 'I found that joke in my stocking. If it happens again, I'll change laundry's.'"

Bob's new straight *man*, Louise Troxell, would say "I just came back from the doctor." Then Bob would ask "Well, what about that?" Then she'd say, "Well, the doctor said I'd have to go to the mountains for my kidneys."

"That's too bad," Bob said. "Yes," she answered, I didn't even know they were up there."

Now it was on to New York for the new act and Les confidently drifts into the B.F. Keith office without an appointment:

"Here I am,"

"Who are you?"

"I'm Bob Hope."

"Who's Bob Hope?"

Here it is, exactly as it happened, according to Bob, the historic change from Les Hope to *Bob Hope*. Les thought *Bob* generated more *"Hi ya, fellers!"* type of personality. It just sounded right. Goodbye, Les; hello, *Bob*!

Now, New York, New York had to be conquered. The Keith's Jefferson Theater and their giant- sized Proctor's Eighty Sixth Street were surely the right venues to practice his talents and introduce his new comedy ideas. A contract led to performances at the coveted Albee Theater in Downtown Brooklyn. Louise and Bob were declared the best of the new acts.

"One joke, however, staged with Louise, got me into a little trouble. It was at Keith's in Chicago. She walks on and says, 'Boy, you're sure an attractive fellow,' and I said, 'Yes, I come from a very brave family. My brother slapped the gangster Al Capone in the face.'"

"Your brother *slapped* Al Capone in the face?" Louise asked, shocked.

"Yes,"

"I'd like to meet him and shake his hand."

"Now my big punch line, *'We're not going to dig him up just for that!'*"

Cast of "Roberta". Bob, Ray Middleton, Tamara, Sydney Greenstreet *(R. Grudens collection)*

Capone was the crime czar of Chicago at the time. To avoid problems, the stage manager urged Bob to take out the joke, but he refused. At the Bismarck hotel where Bob and Louise stayed, Bob received a phone call the following Sunday morning. The caller *urged* Bob to take out the joke asking, "Are you the one doing the Al Capone joke at the Keith's? If you are, do us a favor and remove it and we'll be around to thank you." He hung up saying he was just "one of the boys."

End of very funny Al Capone joke.

The death knell—the sledge-hammer blow—for vaudeville was looming in the presence of talking movies. Vaudeville stars heading for Hollywood was enough proof. Vaudeville surfaced as an entertainment contender about 1883. It finally withered and died in 1932. Some say it didn't die, but merely changed its form and moved on.

The word was that vaudeville became sick; its trouble was creeping atrophy of the box office muscles induced by the twin viruses, talking movies and radio.

VARIETY, the show business newspaper, opined:

"The tendency of middle class people to go to the moving pictures has caused some uneasiness, but we are still of the same opinion, after long observation, that was expressed in these columns months ago, viz.: that the moving picture cannot supersede vaudeville or burlesque."

Columbia Records A & R man Mitch Miller declared the same sort of negative prediction in the 1950s about exploding rock & roll's ability to replace standard music forms and traditional performing. How wrong was he?

Bob spent about thirteen years in vaudeville, the experience enriching him with a few lessons in free enterprise that included thrift, self-reliance, and innovation.

By this time, Bob was initiated into the Broadway scene appearing as bandleader Huckleberry Haines in Jerome Kern & Otto Harbach's production of *Roberta*. One of the great song standards Bob introduced, "Smoke Gets In Your Eyes," still holds up today.

"SMOKE GETS IN YOUR EYES"
by Jerome Kern and Otto Harbach

They asked me how I knew
My true love was true
I, of course, replied, something here inside
Cannot be denied.
They said, someday you'll find
All who love are blind
When your heart's on fire
You must realize
Smoke gets in your eyes
So I chaffed them and gayly laughed
To think they could doubt my love
Yet today, my love has flown away
I am without my love
Now, laughing friends deride
Tears I cannot hide
So I smile and say
When the lovely flame dies
Smoke gets in your eyes

THE KISSES OF DOLORES

Young Dolores Reade was singing Harold Arlen's "It's Only a Paper Moon" in a New York nightclub when Bob Hope first saw her in 1933. She closed her act with "Did You Ever See a Dream Walking" moments before she joined him at his table. Dolores liked him instantly. Across the street Bob had a lead in the Broadway show *Roberta*, but Dolores didn't know it.

"I hadn't quite caught his name. I don't think I was really *that* interested, but I found myself asking him to dance. He refused, saying he didn't dance. I figured he was just a chorus boy in the show *Roberta*. Then, actor George Murphy, who was performing in *Roberta* with Bob, asked me to dance. That caused Bob to break in claiming he changed his mind. I took a good look at him and then I knew I liked him, and I thought perhaps he liked me."

Bob and Dolores got together for a bite to eat after Bob's appearance as Huckleberry Haines in *Roberta* and her singing act at the Embassy Club. She promised to see him in his show. Bob did not tell her he was one of the principal stars along with the great English star, Fay Templeton, Ray Middleton (later starred in *Annie Get Your Gun*) Sydney Greenstreet, and actor, later United States Senator, George Murphy, as well as Fred MacMurray. (Imogene Coca was also in it, and Gene Krupa and Glenn Miller were in the orchestra)

....
Bob and Dolores *(photo Van Damm)*
....

"When I got home that first night, my mother asked who I was out with and I told her that I met my future husband, a man in show business and that he was a chorus boy in a show with lots of possibilities. My mother frowned, as she only approved of Irish Catholic men and said that a man like Bob Hope wasn't good enough for me."

Bob experienced emotional highs and lows while appearing in *Roberta*, which accounted for his uncertainty with respect to Dolores. Dolores, however, was closing in on Bob. He didn't concentrate too much on a female partner at that moment in his life, but knew he was attracted to Dolores. Bob's brothers each had already married more than once so he was being extra careful. When Dolores attended Bob's performance, she failed to stop backstage after the show. Bob didn't understand. Puzzled, he went directly to the Embassy Club that evening to find out why she didn't show up.

"I explained that because I was unaware of his major role in the show, I was embarrassed thinking he was only an unimportant chorus boy. Anyway, after explanations, we went out again and promised we would spend that New Year's Eve together."

Bob and Dolores became close at a time when his mother passed away. Bob headed to Cleveland, relieved for his moth-

er and the family. Avis Hope had suffered through a long and difficult illness that slowly sapped her body and mind.

"Mom had no chance with cancer in those days. They kept her from having pain the best way they could. At the end she weighed about seventy-five pounds. But she never gave up. She never was licked."

Avis Hope had favored Bob above the other boys, always defending his decisions to remain in show business no matter how bad things were for him at one time or another, especially when he would call his mother for comfort and advice.

" My mother waged a campaign against my seeing Bob. Some newspaper columnists gossiped about Bob's other female relationships. When I asked him about the tabloid notices, he denied them, saying they were items of the past. With that out of the way, and promises made to one another, we drove to Erie, Pennsylvania—a favorite town I loved—and we got married. Bob only lost two days from *Roberta* We were married on February 19th and promptly set up housekeeping in a furnished apartment and I set to helping Bob grow in his career."

Her first effort was to encourage Bob to find a worthy agent, one who handled important clients and knew how and where to place talented performers. She felt that agents had contacts and knew the ropes. Although Bob was brash and harshly direct promoting his show business career, he lacked the basic knowledge of managing his own fledgling career. He needed direction and better bookings. *Roberta*, however, opened the door to his future.

In 1936 Bob performed once again on Broadway in a Shubert Brothers show *The Ziegfeld Follies* cast with Eve Arden; the star, the legendary Fannie Brice; and the exotic Josephine Baker. Bob sang "I Can't Get Started," a song that has remained the number one song of the era in surveys taken even today, but it's the big band version recorded by Bunny Berigan, playing trumpet, and doing the vocals on this classic tune, that prevails.

"I CAN'T GET STARTED"
by Vernon Duke and Ira Gershwin

I've flown around the world in a plane
I've settled revolutions in Spain
The North Pole I have charted
But I can't get started with you

Around the golf course I'm under par
And all the movies want me to star
I've got a house, a showplace
But I get no-place with you

You're so supreme,
Lyrics I write of you,
Scheme
Just for the sight of you
Dream
Both day and night of you
And what good does it do?

In nineteen twenty-nine I sold short
In England I'm presented at court,
But, you've got me downhearted
'Cause I can't get started with you.

Cole Porter's Broadway musical *Red, Hot, & Blue*, followed *Follies* in the fall of 1936 and starred Ethel Merman, Jimmy Durante, and Bob Hope. Bob was mischievous on this show. It seems that almost every night he would come up on stage with Merman and Durante, and carelessly toss a funny line and the others would grasp at it and even funnier things would happen. They would toss out lines to others in the show, strictly ad-libbing and everyone had lots of fun. Bob sang "It's

De-Lovely" one of Porter's show stopping songs. Bob still loves to sing that song today.

IT'S DE- LOVELY
by Cole Porter

The night is young, the skies are clear,
So if you want to go walking, dear,
It's delightful, it's delicious, it's de-lovely.
I understand the reason why
You're sentimental, 'cause so am I,
It's delightful, it's delicious, it's de-lovely.
You can tell at a glance
What a swell night this is for romance
You can hear dear Mother Nature murmuring low
"Let yourself go."
So please be sweet, my chickadee,
And when I kiss you, just say to me,
"It's delightful, it's delicious,
"It's delectable, it's delirious,
It's dilemma, it's delimit, it's deluxe,
It's De-lovely.

....

The Great
Durante, Ethel
Merman and
Bob in "Red,
Hot and Blue!",
1937 *(photo
Van Damm)*

....

Bob and his
gals from
"Ziegfeld
Follies" 1936
(Eve Arden on
lower left)
*(courtesy Movie
Star News)*

When Bob's father died the following Spring, while he was in Red, Hot and Blue, Bob wrapped up his association with vaudeville and Broadway.

"My father died of all kinds of complications when he was sixty-six. That, even in those days was not old. He was a very strong man. Being a stonemason doesn't breed weaklings, but he just gave up. He'd been knocked off his pins when Ma'am died, and never got used to living alone."

Then, along came radio.

With Mary Jane Saunders. A scene from Sorrowful Jones *(courtesy Paramount Pictures)*

LEE GORDON *presents*—

Bob HOPE

BOB HOPE, in a scene from his starring picture, "THE SEVEN LITTLE FOYS"

in the "BIG SHOW"
2ND AUSTRALIAN TOUR 1955

★★★★★★★★★★★★★★★★★★★★★★★★★★★★★★★★

ACT THREE:
RADIO-MOVIES-TELEVISION
DON'T TOUCH THAT DIAL

"Bob On the Air Hope" 1951 *(courtesy NBC)*

Bob on NBC Radio 1935 *(courtesy NBC)*

DON'T TOUCH THAT DIAL

"You Remember Radio. TV without eye strain"

As the great radio comedian Fred Allen once declared:

> *Radio was the first free entertainment ever given to the public. It was piped into the home as a service similar to running water. When the novelty of the shows wore off many people had more respect for running water than they did for radio.*

Bob Hope's voice penetrated radio in 1934, soon after starring in Broadway's *Ziegfeld Follies*. Within ten short years, Bob's show became radio's number one show. (NBC and CBS were then battling for the number one position among 900 other radio stations across the country) *Fibber Magee and Molly* stood at number two, and Walter Winchell (Your New York Daily Mirror News Correspondent) tied with *The Jack Benny Program* for third place. Bob had just returned from his USO world tours.

His first radio efforts were as a guest on the *Major Bowes Hour* and Rudy Vallee's *The Fleischman Hour*. Vaudeville performers who turned to radio had to learn to lower their voices. A good example: song-belter Al Jolson always shouted out his songs in large theaters due to the absence of a microphone (which had not been invented yet) and the need to be heard everywhere in a theater. All had to learn to utilize a "mike." Bing Crosby and Frank Sinatra were microphone pioneers, so to speak, arriving on the scene at just the right time, embracing it and lightly crooning into it for a more intimate effect. Crooners like Crosby and Sinatra could not have been effective without a "mike."

BOB: "I used to get the money and run into a corner and count it. I felt I was stealing it. I couldn't believe anyone could make so much money talking into a microphone."

On Bob's radio show few listeners could forget the hilarious spoof of two very ugly debutantes, comediennes Brenda and Cobina, played by Elvia Allman and Blanche Stewart, on Bob's radio show in the late 1930's. People sat in their living rooms to hear the same kind of comedy they used to hear in vaudeville houses:

Cobina: *I can't wait for Bob and Skinnay Ennis to get here. I'm shaking all over like I got PARSLEY! Do you think they'll go for my lovely long eyebrows?*
Brenda: *Of course, but I think you'd look prettier if you combed them back over your head to hide your bald spot.*
Cobina: *Good idea.*

Now, Bob's agent, dynamic Louis "Doc" Shurr, garnered Bob a coveted spot on T*he Bromo Seltzer Intimate Hour* and provided a sidekick, Patricia (Honey Chile) Wilder who became Bob's *Gracie Allen*. Patricia was young, pretty and soft spoken, unlike the usual vaudeville foil. The show didn't do well so Bob returned briefly to the stage.

Honey Chile, the dumb dora style foil for Bob always garnered laughs on the ill-fated Bromo Seltzer program:

BOB: "You know, Honey Chile, there are a lot of comedians on the air. Why did you pick me for your partner?"
HONEY CHILE:" 'Cause ah had a fight with mah folks and ah want to do somethin' to disgrace 'em."

Then, while filming the movie *The Big Broadcast of 1938*, his first starring feature, he signed in New York with *The Woodbury Show*. It originated from Hollywood with a live audience in attendance, which made Bob more comfortable. Then 35 years old, Bob signed with his soon to be signature weekly radio show sponsored by Pepsodent Tooth Paste and hired his first batch of writers—seven in all. The show lasted until 1950.

Like his work in vaudeville, Bob worked very hard to become radio's premier performer. The Pepsodent show always featured popular guest stars and vocalists. Female vocalists Judy Garland and Doris Day were regulars on Bob's radio show.

Bob: "That was great, Judy. But tell me, how do you feel about becoming a cast member of my show?"
Judy: "Oh, I'm really happy to be here, Mr. Hope. You know my schoolteacher's happy I'm on your program, too. She

says I ought to be happy to take *anything* to get started."

Bob: "But Judy, are you sure you'll feel at home on this program?"

Judy: "Oh, yes, Mr. Hope. You should have seen the strange creatures I worked with in 'The Wizard of Oz.'"

Bob: "Judy, I want us to get along on this show. I want you to treat me as a father. When you get a little older, you can treat me as a brother....and when you get a little older than that, it's every man for himself."

Bob and Judy, 1940 *(courtesy NBC)*

Judy Garland appeared often with Bob on "Command Performances," a radio show geared for servicemen during the war, notably on Christmas Day, 1943, on the Elgin Watch Show with Bing, Bob, Lena Horne, Carmen Miranda, and a host of others, a two-hour salute to those overseas and for workers on the home front. In February, 1945 on a gala production of "Dick Tracy" which featured Bob, Bing, Jimmy Durante, Dinah Shore, and Frank Sinatra, Judy was also a featured player.

Bob began the *Pepsodent Show* in the old NBC Hollywood studios on September 27, 1938, in front of a live audience. He guided the left-over audience from the *Edgar Bergen-Charlie McCarthy* radio show from the adjacent studio into his studio believing firmly that a live studio audience would insure the show's success. Bob knew Bergen from *Follies* days. Bergen had been fired from the *Follies* and moved into radio. Bob felt badly for him at the time:

Bob: "Radio! Nobody will be able to see the dummy on your lap"

Bergen: "Yeah, but nobody will be able to see me moving my lips, either."

In short order, Bergen's show became the top show on radio.

Comedian Jerry "Professor "Colonna became Bob's zany comedy foil on the Pepsodent program. In those days a single sponsor usually sustained each show allowing it to be frequently named after the sponsor. *(Lux Presents Hollywood, The Jell-O Program, The Chase & Sanborn Hour, The Chesterfield Supper Club, The Kraft Music Hall, etc)* Bob's persona, like Jack Benny's, was orchestrated to have him appear self deprecating, cowardly and egotistical, and additionally, characterized as a skirt chaser. This formula assured Bob's success in the public eye and kept listeners tuning in. Add the phony Jack Benny-Fred Allen style feud with Bing Crosby, and Bob's show ascended quickly to the top of the charts.

*****

Colonna: "Hope, I'm calling you from San Francisco. I'm
    walking on air over the Golden Gate Bridge."
Hope: "Professor, no human being can walk on air!"
Colonna: "They can't?"
Hope: "No!"(sound effect: slide whistle down...loud splash.)
Colonna: "You hadda open your big mouth!"

*****

In 1945 Bob signed with Lever Brothers (soap company) to a lucrative ten year contract, but it lasted only five, Bob leaving because Lever Brothers' constantly interfered with his comedy material: to Bob, unacceptable.

Just as Bob's live USO overseas shows earned him eternal fame among millions of servicemen, radio contributed the same for stateside fame and fortune. As the Pepsodent show's popularity climbed, war loomed in Europe. America felt war couldn't happen here. Radio shows proliferated and rating wars surfaced in radio then as it exists in television today.

The *Bob Hope Pepsodent Show* became the number one radio show in America, starring America's number one comedian, leaving established shows featuring Jack Benny and Fred Allen in the dust. It opened with Bob's monolog, and included skits, exchanges with his regular cast and a guest star, like Crosby, and a Doris Day or Margaret Whiting song or two.

"Of course, the people I used to sell Pepsodent to are now using Polident."

Top: Bob
with Frances
Langford and
Jerry Colonna
Bottom:
Bob with
Jane Russell
(courtesy NBC)

On the evening of December 9, 1941, NBC Radio broke in and announced: "The Bob Hope Pepsodent Show will not be heard tonight." The Japanese had attacked Pearl Harbor two days earlier. The utilization of radio reporting during wartime would change the way we received our news and entertainment forever and would bring forth, front and center, radio with images: an interloper named television stood in the shadows. Meanwhile, Hollywood beckoned and Bob eagerly responded.

Bob and Doris
Day, 1945
(courtesy NBC)

SEARCHING FOR OSCARS

*"I arrived in Hollywood carrying
a log-sized chip on my shoulder."*

Bob's enterprising agent, Doc Shurr, first signed him with a two-reeler producer, Paramount Pictures, with studios in Astoria, New York, for six film comedy shorts at $2,500.00 each. Bob's first real film, a short, was entitled *Paree, Paree*, wherein Bob introduced the now standard evergreen "You Do Something to Me," composed by the prolific Cole Porter:

"YOU DO SOMETHING TO ME"
by Cole Porter

You do something to me,
Something that simply mystifies me.
Tell me, why should it be
You have the pow'r to hypnotize me?
Let me live 'neath your spell,
You do that voodoo that you do so well,
For you do something to me
That nobody else can do.

The first film starring Bob, *The Big Broadcast of 1938*, established him as a major film star. Co-stars were W.C. Fields, Martha Raye, and Lynne Overman. Bob crooned his future theme song "Thanks for the Memory" to contract player Shirley Ross in a nostalgic style duet that stole the show, and was truly the highlight of the film. Bob's phrasing and smooth delivery is excellent and still evokes tears from many of us.

The song won an Academy Award and became Bob's first hit record, although his first commercial recording was a 78 RPM Liberty Records recording of "It's De-Lovely."

"Thanks for the Memory" as performed by Bob and Shirley is recognized as one of the tenderest and best expressed songs to come out of a Hollywood film.

"THANKS FOR THE MEMORY"

by Ralph Rainger and Leo Robin

As performed in the film by
Bob Hope and Shirley Ross

Thanks for the memory,
Of rainy afternoons
Swinging Harlem tunes,
And motor trips and burning lips,
And burning toast and prunes,
How lovely it was.

Thanks for the memory
Of candlelight and wine,
Castles on the Rhine,
The Parthenon and moments on
The Hudson River Line.
How lovely it was.

Many's the time that we feasted,
And many's the time that we fasted,
Oh, well, it was swell while it lasted,
We did have fun,
And no harm done

So, thanks for the memory
Of crap games on the floor,
Nights in Singapore
You might have been a headache
But you never were a bore,
Ah, thank you so much.

Thanks for the memory,
Of China's funny wall,
Transatlantic calls,
That weekend at Niagara
When we hardly saw the falls.
Thank you so much.

(Music only)...for the memory
Of lunch from twelve to four,
Sunburn at the shore,
That pair of gay pajamas
That you bought and never wore,
(Say, by the way, what did happen to those pajamas?)

All those sweet secrets,
That couldn't be put in a day wire,
Too Bad it all had to go haywire,
That's life I guess,

I love...your dress,
(Do you?)
(It's pretty!)
(Thanks!)

(Thanks)—for the memory,
Of faults that you forgave,
Rainbows on a wave,
And stockings in the basement
When a fellow needs a shave,
Ah, thank you so much.
(Laughter, giggling, embracing)

Thanks for the Memory
Of gardens at Versailles,
And beef and kidney pie,
The night you worked
And then came home
With lipstick on your tie,
(How lovely that was..)
(Huh?)

(Music only)—for the memory
Of lingerie with lace
Yes, and Pilsner by the case,
And how I jumped
The day you trumped
My one and only ace.
How lovely that was,

We said goodbye with a highball
And I got as high as a steeple
(Did ya?)
But we were intelligent people,
No tears—no fuss
Hurray for us (sung together)

Thanks for the memory, (Music only)
Strictly entre' nous
(between us)
Darling, how are you?
And how are all those little dreams
That never did come true,
Awfully glad I met you
Cheeri-o and toodle-oo

Thank you.
Thank you !
(Oh! Bud.)
(I know, darling, I know, dear!)

Bob was particularly happy to share billing with comedian W.C. Fields, whose efforts he always admired. Further, he was able to work alongside Jack Benny, Bing Crosby(eventually in all the seven *Road* films), Gary Cooper, Martha Raye, Mae West, and George Burns and Gracie Allen. After *The Big Broadcast of 1938*, Bob became an equally significant member of the Paramount Studios stable of stars.

Bob Hope and
Shirley Ross
*(courtesy
Paramount
Pictures)*

Bob performed in a string of films following *Broadcast* including a follow-up film with Shirley Ross entitled *Thanks for the Memory*, due to the success of *Broadcast*. The song written for that film, "Two Sleepy People" became another Hope song success.

"TWO SLEEPY PEOPLE"
by Hoagy Carmichael and Frank Loesser

Here we are, out of cigarettes
Holding hands and yawning
See how late it gets
Two sleepy people
By dawn's early light
Too much in love
To say, 'Goodnight'.
Here we are, in the cozy chair,
Picking on a wishbone
From the Frigidaire,
Two sleepy people
With nothing to say,
And too much in love to break away.

Do you remember the nights
We used to linger in the hall?

Father didn't like you at all
Do you remember the reason
We married in the fall?
To rent this little nest
And get a bit of rest.
Well, here we are
Just about the same,
Foggy little feller
Drowsy little dame
Two sleepy people
By dawn's early light,
And too much in love
To say goodnight.

Bob Hope's beautiful Palm Springs, California home and swimming pool. *(courtesy Mitoch & Sons)*

About that time Bob and Dolores built their first home in Toluca Lake, California, paying $6,000 dollars for a three acre plot, and Bob hired his first writer for a radio show, fully sponsored by Lucky Strike cigarettes.

Here, Bob introduced his newly developed, sturdy form of topical comedy. Although the show eventually was canceled, it paved the way for his long-running Pepsodent radio show. Melville Shavelson and Milt Josefsberg were his first choice for his new group of comedy writers. The addition of Melvin Frank and Norman Panama formed "Hope's Army" of come-

Bob Hope's Palm Springs Home

dy writers. Radio, unlike vaudeville, voraciously gobbled up comedy material on a weekly basis, thus the need for help in the form of writers.

Mel: "If you could make the fellers whose jobs depended on their not laughing, laugh, then Bob would check off the jokes that went into the show. That's when I developed my first ulcer."

Bob: "I keep an earthquake emergency kit in my house. It's filled with food, water, and a half a dozen gag writers."

Bob first used his *signature* tune, "Thanks for the Memory" as a theme on the Pepsodent show, backed by Skinnay Ennis' band.

The first *Road* picture, *The Road to Mandalay* featured Dorothy Lamour along with Bing and Bob:

Dorothy Lamour: *"Over the next twenty years we did seven films. It was fun from the very first day. We were all exuberant about the first one. We never dreamed it would be so successful and last so long, although sometimes the boys drove me crazy with their zany tricks."*

Bob eventually appeared in fifty-four feature films, aside from shorts and cameos. Most were formula comedies and some were *serious* comedies. A complete listing follows the text in this book. When I first interviewed Bob, I remarked that the film *Cat and the Canary* frightened me when my mother first took me to see it. I was an impressionable seven year old and had nightmares for a week.

"It scared the hell out of me, too!" retorted Bob. We broke up.

(courtesy Paramount Pictures)

"Star Spangled Revue" poster, 1950 *(photo Library of Congress)*

T.V. Takes With...

Sid Caesar and Imogene Coca
(NBC Archives)

Arnold Palmer and Dean Martin
(NBC Archives)

Ed Sullivan *(NBC Archives)*

Jack Benny *(NBC Archives)*

The *Cat and the Canary* was a planned film designed specifically for Bob and co-starred Paulette Goddard, establishing Bob as one of the industry's strongest crowd magnets and producing a ten year contract for Goddard at Paramount. The film represented the first time Bob combined all he had learned from his vaudeville and Broadway days, establishing his persona for all future work in films and television. The success of that film led to a sort of sequel in The *Ghost Breakers* also co-starring Goddard, Paul Lukas and future superstar Anthony Quinn.

Significantly, Bob's most popular film *The Paleface*, a western spoof with Jane Russell appearing as the legendary Calamity Jane and Bob as traveling correspondence school dentist Painless Peter Potter, broke all box-office records. Bob sang the Academy Award winning song "Buttons & Bows."

"BUTTONS AND BOWS"
by Jay Livingston and Ray Evans

East is east and west is west
And the wrong one I have chose
Let's go where you'll keep on wearing
Those frills and flowers and buttons and bows,
Rings and things and buttons and bows
Don't bury me on the lone prairie
Take me where the cement grows
Let's move down to some big town
Where they love a gal by the cut o' her clothes
And you'll stand out in buttons and bows
I'll love you in buckskins
Or skirts that you've homespun
But I'll love ya longer, stronger
Where your friends don't tote a gun
My bones denounce, the buckboards bounce
And the cactus hurts my toes,
Let's vamoose where gals keep usin' those
Silks and satins and linen that shows,
And I'm all yours in buttons and bows.

Catching TV Viewers

*"...Television....you can now go blind
in six delicious flavors.."*

**".....I'm glad to be back on radio. It seems to
have so much more to offer than television...things
like money...but I like television....I have one of
those sets with a screen so small you have to sit
right next to it. Last night during dinner Hopalong
Cassidy lassoed three of my boiled potatoes...and
all during dinner I had to keep Milton Berle's
hand out of my soup..."**

When Bob was filming *The Road to Rio* at Paramount, the
studio formed a television station of its own, and on January
22, 1947 it presented a special program to a very limited television audience. Bob emceed, while Cecil B. De Mille was the
producer. It featured Dorothy Lamour, Ann Rutherford, Bill
Demarest, and Jerry Colonna, as well as the singing DeCastro
Sisters.

Bob: "When vaudeville died, television was the box they put it
in, and those TV lights were very hot. You sweated all the
way through. Someone had to change that, and, thank
goodness they did."

Bob Hope's network television debut began on NBC,
twelve years after he started on NBC radio. Television had
arrived for Bob whose radio fans could now see as well as hear
him perform. Some of his future sponsors were Fortune Five
Hundred companies: Chrysler, Ford, GM, Texaco, Timex, and
Pepsodent.

**"All I know about television is that I want to get into it as
soon as possible—before Milton Berle uses up all my jokes."**

Bob's first TV effort occurred before a Paramount
Television camera on Easter Sunday in April, 1950, high up on
the roof of the New Amsterdam Theater on 42nd Street, an
early, but regular NBC television studio. This milestone set the
tone for future telecasts. Sponsor Frigidaire paid the unGodly

sum of $40,000 to Bob alone. The show, "Star Spangled Revue" also featured English music hall star Bea Lillie, swashbuckling actor Douglas Fairbanks, Jr., and Dinah Shore, who sang Johnny Mercer's "Baby It's Cold Outside." Total production cost: $125,000.00. The handwriting was on the wall.

"This is Bob 'First Commercial Television Broadcast' Hope telling you gals who have tuned me in...and I wanna make this emphatic...If my face isn't handsome and debonair...It isn't me...It's the static!"

"It's amazing how many people see you on TV. I did my first TV show a month ago and the next day five million television sets were sold. The people who couldn't sell theirs..... threw them away."

If radio created a star in Bob Hope, it was television that elevated him to superstar. Always in the right place at the right time: vaudeville, radio, USO trips, movies, television; Bob was able to overcome the major problems he encountered in each medium as he progressed. Fortunately, the public always seemed to favor and enjoy his vaudeville and Broadway ventures, as well as his radio and TV shows, allowing him to outlast many big names, with even bigger shows, in all mediums.

On television, Bob realized that being more relaxed by abandoning the rapid-fire monologue delivery he used on radio, and appearing to be visually more casual, worked better for him. The proof: Bob's 1970 and 1971 Christmas Specials achieved the highest Nielsen rating score ever for television specials up to that time. He had adjusted to television quite nicely.

Bob's 1958 television special filmed in Russia spawned many good jokes:

"Russian television viewers are a lot like Americans. They're crazy about Westerns. There's only one difference. They root for the Indians."

"The Kremlin walls encloses churches, museums, government offices, and the Grand Palace, where the Communist Party meets. It's hard to describe, but it looks like Charles Addams' answer to the Pentagon."

"And if you want to bring a romantic tear to your girl's eye, send her a box of candy. They have a picture of a hydro-electric plant on the cover."

Backing up a bit, it was Bob who introduced the later, widely used *cue cards*, large cardboard scripts held high above and behind the camera written in large type from which Bob could easily read. It avoided memorizing scripts. He also learned to use them effectively while on his overseas tours. Even there, it beat holding scripts in his hand as he once did during radio shows.

During 1953, Bob's Monday night television program became the very first full hour color TV show. RCA-NBC had won the color TV wars by presenting their compatible, all electronic television system on a closed-circuit field test on October 26, 1951, and demonstrated in the viewing rooms of the then RCA Exhibition Hall on West 49th Street. It was a secret competition eventually won over Columbia's color wheel system. I attended that historical demonstration show that featured exotic singer Yma Sumac, Broadway star Nanette Fabray, and George Burton and his Birds, from a third floor studio. I recall the cameras being much larger and designed differently than the cameras used for black & white screens. I also remember the colors *running* across the small screen. That problem was soon solved.

Bob's fabulous television career ran the gamut of his variety of acts, acts he performed during vaudeville days, radio days and even Broadway days. He actually re-created the show *Roberta* with Howard Keel and Janis Paige on one of his specials. During his run of specials, Bob elevated the sagging careers of Frank Sinatra, who duly acknowledged the help from Bob, and Zsa-Zsa Gabor, as well as a number of sports figures and individuals by having them appear on his widely watched shows.

When he took the cameras with him on some of the USO shows and NBC featured them on specials for the people at home, his stature rose even higher. Bob had turned television into his own personal vaudeville circuit.

One of Bob's great TV shows was the *Texaco Special* on October 24, 1975. A two-hour show composed of old segments from Bob's twenty-five previous years on television and included almost one-hundred stars in both black and white and color. John Wayne, Bing Crosby, and Frank Sinatra appeared live. All Bob's legendary guests re-appeared on video film. To list a few: Ginger Rogers, Jimmy Durante, Milton Berle, Jimmy Cagney, Lucille Ball, Steve Allen, Barbra Streisand, Natalie Wood, Perry Como, and so many others. The show was a rousing success. Press notices were all positive. The parade of stars, old and new, stole the hearts of millions. It was a superior TV show. Bob became a performer of great merit and was declared to be a great humanitarian, and a very funny man, indeed!

On February 3, 1980, a six-hour, seven- night retrospective of Bob's more than 30 years of entertaining at military bases and hospitals in the U.S. and overseas began on NBC television.

....

Hope performs for audience at USO in Fairbanks, Alaska. September 1942 *(courtesy USO)*
....

ACT FOUR:
WITH GOLF'S GREATS

AND AMATEURS

"Here's how you do it, Bing." *(courtesy Paramount Pictures)*

Left to Right: Bob, Tricia Nixon, Patricia Nixon, President Gerald Ford, Dolores Hope, President Nixon, Betty Ford, Henry Kissinger and Arnold Palmer. *(Arnold Palmer collection)*

"I love playing golf with the pros, Ben Hogan, Arnold Palmer, Sam Snead, and Jack Nicklaus. After all, golf is my real profession, entertainment is just a sideline. I tell jokes to pay my greens fees."

Mention golf and Bob Hope brightens up like a 1000 watt halogen light bulb. Bob has played golf with so many celebrities that he had to write a book just to accommodate the list of players and the great games they played together over the years. His interest in golf began in his vaudeville days when shows were at night and there was time to spare during the day. And, remember, Bob was once a caddy. He learned the rudiments of the game while carrying other golfers clubs as a youngster back in Cleveland.

ARNOLD PALMER

The first time Bob Hope saw Arnold Palmer play was in the mid-50s.

"When Arnie hit the ball the Earth shook. The man radiated raw power. When I asked him later on if he'd mind working on my game, he smiled that natural Pennsylvania smile and said, 'I've already seen your game, Bob. I think it would be a good idea if you took up tennis.'"

Arnold Palmer, one of golf's greats, is actually a longtime friend of Bob, thanks to their mutual interest in the game. Their relationship stretches over 40 years. Arnie and Bob quickly became friends playing together in the sport that Bob loves best and Arnie plays better. Arnie is a five time winner of the "Bob Hope Desert Classic Pro-Am Tournament" and a favorite golf venue for him:

One year, when I was there in the desert to play in the tournament during the Nixon years, the President asked Bob and me to take a quick trip in a Marine helicopter to his Western White House at San Clemente for what was later dubbed a 'mini summit' meeting.

We joined the President, Secretary of State Henry Kissinger, Vice President Gerald Ford and several other national security people to discuss ways of ending the Vietnam War.

I wasn't sure why I was brought into the discussions, but when President Nixon asked me what I thought should be done, I paused for a second, looked askance at Bob sitting there with anticipation, and then said something like: "If the decision were mine, I guess I wouldn't pussyfoot around. Let's get things over with as quickly as possible, for everybody's sake. Why not go for the green?"

Bob was certainly glad he brought his golfing partner and friend with him to the meeting. Bob would have invoked the same opinion—in different words perhaps, as there was no room for comedy there.

Bob had Arnie appear on a couple of his television shows during the 1960s and set him up as a straight man with jokes like this:

BOB: "Arnie, how come you never invited me to appear on your show, *Challenge Golf?*"
ARNIE: "We don't do comedy, Bob."
BOB: "I mean—*just* to play golf!"
ARNIE: "We don't do comedy, Bob!"

When Bob invited Arnold Palmer to perform a cameo role in the film *Call Me Bwana*, he readily accepted for the fun of it. But, Bob had to convince him to travel to Kenya, Africa, where it was to be filmed but where the political situation was unsettled at the time. Arnie wasn't exactly enthusiastic. Then, instead, the producers decided to shoot the picture outside of London, England, at Pinewood Studios, so Arnold agreed.

ARNIE: "We shot the segment in a studio in London. In the scene I pop my head into a tent looking for a stray ball I had supposedly hit, which Bob, eating breakfast, mistakes for a poached egg in a cup (where it landed) and tries to crack it open. I played it straight again to Bob's usual quips. My line was, 'Anybody seen my ball in here?' I didn't expect an Academy Award."

BOB: "'Then there was the golf sequence where Arnie and I hit balls in the midst of what was meant to be a jungle clearing. We'd practice during a break in the shooting and then Arnie would put on a clinic for the crew. He was just great. Great golfer, so-so actor. When Arnie needed to lose some fat, he gave up smoking and embarked on a fitness program. He now only coughs when his opponent is putting."

Arnie was always impressed with Bob Hope's ubiquitous golf motto—"Make sure your golf scoring pencil has an eraser on it."

ARNIE: "Knowing Bob Hope has been a privilege for me."
BOB: "Ditto."

JACK NICKLAUS

Jack Nicklaus has won more major championships than anyone in golf history. In 1976 Bob played at a pro-am founded by Jack at Muirfield Village in Dublin, Ohio. It was Bob's eightieth birthday and Nicklaus rolled out a cake on the first tee. On each successive tee he had the crowd sing "Happy Birthday" to Bob, who thoroughly enjoyed the surprise.

Once, Jack Nicklaus drove the green on the 7th hole at Scioto, a hole that measured 371 yards with a slight dogleg. He drove the green and sank the putt for an eagle.

BOB: How come I can't hit the ball like that?
JACK: You'd get more distance if you took the head covers off your woods.
BOB: You stick to golf. I'll tell the jokes.

Jack Nicklaus played his first professional tournament in the 1962 Los Angles Open. His pay check was a whopping $33.33. He's done a little better since then.

BOB: "Developing an image with the public is harder than Sainthood. Saints don't have to sign autographs. They just have to perform miracles, and Nicklaus does that every time he swings a golf club."

JACK: Most people are unaware of the fact that Bob Hope was once a pretty good golfer. I played in a pro-am with him and he shot a 73 on his own ball. I've also played with Bob when you wondered if he would break 100. But to Bob it just didn't matter, because he has never really cared about how well he played. Bob simply loves the game and loves playing it.

Perhaps, more importantly, Bob was always there to enjoy the day, graciously endeavoring to entertain everyone, or sometimes just to help out a needy charity. That, among many other reasons, is what makes Bob a great guy.

Ever the entertainer, Bob always had a story to tell and sometimes re-tell. Playing in as many as 150 different charity events a year at one point in his career, Bob was always playing to a fresh audience who always laughed, as did I. With every line he delivered, not once did Bob offend anyone. It was always a case of good, clean fun.

Bob and I spent much time together playing golf, including at a number of charity events. He is someone I have admired and respected for the more than 40 years I have known him. And, publicly or privately, the consistency of his personality is always the same. As we all know, Bob has always loved being on stage, even if that stage was a golf course. But, whether on stage or at home, Bob's persona remains the same—a good man, a good friend. I have been fortunate to say I have known him as both.

Jack Nicklaus with Bob at 1986 Phoenix open. *(Exclusive photo Lissa Wales)*

When Bob first began his fund-raising Bob Hope Desert Classic Pro-Am Golf Tournament in 1959, that draws up to 110, 000 spectators and runs 90 holes in five days, he never envisioned it would provide the money to construct the Eisenhower Medical Center in Palm Desert, California. Millions of dollars, earned by Bob, have been poured into his and Dolores' favorite project. Bob also donated the eighty acres on which it was built, a real testimonial to Bob's unselfishness in his quest to help those who need help, from those able to give help. Bob and Dolores donate major annual funds to The Society of Singers in Los Angeles, an active association of show business professionals and related individuals. It's roster is a *who's who* of show business.

Bob's golfing partner, Bing Crosby, also supported a charitable fund- raising golf tournament at Pebble Beach, near San Francisco.

"Bing and I had lots of fun playing golf all over the world. As you will remember, Bing actually died on a golf course. He was a really sensational golfer, and a pretty good singer too, some say."

During the 1950s, sports lovers Bob and Bing owned shares in Major League baseball teams. For Bing, it was part ownership in the Pittsburgh Pirates franchise and for Bob it was ownership in the Cleveland Indians:

"I really get a kick being one of the owners of the Indians. There's only one thing wrong. Since I started backing the Indians, Roy Rogers won't talk to me anymore. Even his horse Trigger turns his back. And, I still have to sneak into the stadium to watch the games. In the first inning of one game, I yelled, 'Throw the bum out.' and they did."

Bob also maintained an interest in the Los Angeles Rams Football team.

Of course, Jack Nicklaus and Arnold Palmer still play golf today. Bob has given it up for the moment. At this writing Jack Nicklaus was playing in England, competing in the Senior British Open.

Jack came in 3rd.

JERRY VALE & JOE TORRE

"Yankees Manager Joe Torre and I were playing a really slow game of golf when a ball lands over our heads as we were teeing off."

"Who is that?" asks Joe Torre, "I know we are slow, but, really."

"Here they come, now!" said Jerry

"Hey, it's Bob Hope! And someone is with him. Isn't that General Schwarzkopf?".

"You're right," said Jerry, who is thrilled.

"Hey guys, how about we join up with you for a foursome?" said Bob.

The quartet now organized, the game moves on.

"Jerry, What do you shoot....108?" asked Bob.

"Well, Bob, I'm not having a good game today, but that's all."

Play goes on. Everyone enjoying the game, including all the small talk.

General Schwarzkopf wedges up from the rough to within five feet of the cup.

"Oh, that's good. That's close enough," says genial Bob to the General.

"What does that mean—'close enough,'" asks Torre, scratching his head and lifting his hat, as the General picks up his ball and moves on towards the next tee.

"He's a General. You give him what he wants." says Bob in a matter-of-fact tone as he moves on following General Schwarzkopf's lead.

Bob tosses a smile over his shoulder to Torre and Vale.

"That's show business," grins Jerry Vale.

Torre just shrugged.

Bing, Bob and Dottie Lamour backstage *(courtesy Paramount Pictures)*

★★★★★★★★★★★★★★★★★★★★★★★★★★★★★★

ACT FIVE:
BOB'S TWO LEGENDS

BING CROSBY AND LES BROWN

BING CROSBY—
FORTY FIVE YEARS OF FUN

"When you work with Bing, you always look great."

Bing: "Sorry I'm late, Bob. I had trouble finding a place to park."

Bob: "What do you mean? The stable's right outside."

Bing: "Is that what that was? I thought it was your dressing room. It was—the last time I was on your show."

*****

Remember Burns and Allen, Abbott & Costello, Fibber Magee and Molly, Lucy and Desi, Dean Martin and Jerry Lewis? Well, I have to inform you that Bob Hope and Bing Crosby's partnership was not quite the same. Theirs was simply an informal marriage of two complex, diverse talents joined together for only special occasions. They didn't appear as a team except during the *Road* films, otherwise maintaining totally separate careers. The offstage friendship was cordial, but never close. Most people assumed the personal side would be much like their association on the screen, but it was actually limited. Bing, an introvert on occasion, and Bob, always an extrovert, didn't hang out together as you may have figured. Under the camera or in front of the mike they had lots of fun working together. Audiences loved them. During all those *Road* films and on their respective radio shows over many years, they meshed beautifully, but mostly kept their professional identities separated from the personal.

Bob Hope attended every possible function, charitable or otherwise, and Bing simply avoided them. When Bing failed to show up for a Friar's Club roast honoring Bob, Bob wondered why he didn't show up. Bing simply said, "I wasn't hungry." Bob always needed to attend and Bing just wasn't generally interested.

Bob, knowing Bing was an easy target for jokes because he was known to be wealthy, (as was Bob) would say things like, "Instead of paying income tax, Bing just calls Washington and asks how much they need."

Bob and Bing on the road *(photo Movie Star News)*

"My world collapsed when I had to hand Bing an Oscar for "Going My Way" when I emceed the Academy Awards in 1944. It was for the best acting performance of the year, knowing in my heart that I should have gotten it for smiling while I handed it to him"

When Bing passed away on a golf course in Spain on October 14, 1977, Bob was stunned. The question of his own mortality, of course, surfaced. He canceled performances for a week. Ward Grant, Bob's press agent, issued this note from Bob the following day:

"The whole world loved Bing with a devotion that not only crossed international boundaries but erased them. He made the world a single place through his music, spoke to it in a language that everybody understands—the language of the heart.

"No matter where you were in the world, because of Bing every Christmas was white, and because we had him with us—it'll always seem a little whiter.

"The world put Bing on a pedestal, but somehow I don't think he ever really knew it. Bing asked the world "Going My Way?" and we all were.

"Yesterday a heart may have stopped, and a voice stilled, but the real melody Bing sang will linger on as long as there is a phonograph to be played....and a heart to be lifted."

Bob was among the very few mourners invited to attend the chapel of St. Paul the Apostle in Los Angeles when Bing Crosby was laid to rest in a hilltop grave near Hollywood. Kathryn Crosby compassionately permitted access to Bob, Rosemary Clooney, and Bing's old friend, bandleader Phil Harris, because she thought it would be insulting to his friends to omit their presence even though Bing's will specified that only his children and wife Kathryn were permitted to attend.

Bob Hope and Bing Crosby met for the first time at New York's Friars Club on 48th Street, the famous show business club that still exists at the same address today. Several months later Bob introduced Bing to audiences on the great stage of the Capitol Theater in New York. Bing had just come off his first major feature film *The Big Broadcast of 1932*, after leaving Paul Whiteman's "King of Jazz" Orchestra, striking out on his own. Bing's hit recording "I Surrender Dear "was riding high. The boys met afterwards at O'Reilly's Bar across from the Capitol and swapped stories, finding plenty to talk about in their respective careers. They even came up with a couple of routines later on worked out while shooting billiards in the Friar's Club game room.

We started to insult each other from the moment we met. I called him the sports shirt that walks like a man...and later...the large, economy size Sinatra..and he *called* me "The man with a nose like a bicycle seat."

Bing: As I live, it's ski snoot.
Bob: Mattress hip.
Bing: Shovel head.
Bob: Blubber.

It's true. I met Bob Hope when I took an engagement at the Capitol Theater in New York. At that juncture, Hope and I hadn't begun to bully each other. That would come later.

Lots of beefs with Robert. He coined the vulgarization "groaner" for the word "crooner." The second time I saw him was at the Paramount. He had caught on and was doing pretty good. Someone came up with the idea of paring us in a picture called The Road to Singapore. As you now know, it worked out fine. Then we appeared on each other's radio shows. Our Hatfield-McCoy "feud" just happened, it was not planned. The abusive dialogue was our kind of fun. Making films, we ad libbed like crazy, violating all the accepted rules. Our antics became accepted by the crew and even the director.

About Hope and golf. We played for the Red Cross over a period stretching from 1941 to 1945 and we would hold a War Bond sale on the 18th green after the match. We auctioned off the balls, our clubs, golf apparel, and anything else we could find. The money always went for bonds. I lost count of the cities and

courses we played on together.

The year 2000 commemorated the Sixtieth anniversary of Bob & Bing's first *Road* film, *Road to Singapore* in 1940. Over the next twenty-two years six more *Road* films were released. 1941 *The Road to Zanzibar*, 1942 *The Road to Morocco*, 1945 *The Road to Utopia*, 1947 *The Road to Rio*, 1952 *The Road to Bali*, and in 1962 it was *The Road to Hong Kong*. Some consider those films to be the most acclaimed comedy series in American film history.

Bob, Dottie and Bing
(courtesy Paramount Pictures)

"I don't know what will happen in our next picture," said Bob at the time, "but anyway, Dorothy Lamour, Bing, and I are having a lot of fun....besides I'm getting a salary for my performance in these *Road* pictures....which, as one critic pointed out, is a perfect example of highway robbery."

"Bing and I never made the two more planned *Road* films. *Road to Moscow* and the *Road to the Fountain of Youth*. We were getting ready to shoot them when Bing got a casting call from Upstairs. He left us on a golf course in the middle of a swing, which was, I suppose, the way he would have preferred. Just a drive and a chip shot to Heaven."

LES BROWN —
SIXTY YEARS OF MUSIC

Traveling with Bob on the tours was very rewarding. We were entertaining our servicemen. It was very important work as far as we were concerned, and my band members got to see parts of the world they wouldn't otherwise have seen. We had people fighting one another to go on those tours. Everyone who went was enthusiastic. They would say: "If so-and-so can't make it, I'll go, just let me know."

Les Brown spent eighteen continuous years overseas with Bob and the USO troupe between December 15 and December 30th, becoming an important part of the legendary Christmas Tours:

Bob always brought the greatest talents and the prettiest girls along. He took a lot of criticism from some folks. And he was never afraid of the dangers we faced. Once, when we flew into Tokyo during the Korean War, I got the news that the Chinese crossed the Yalu River immediately after we left. So I call Bob

Les Brown,
Butch Stone
and Stumpy
Brown at
Keflavik,
Iceland, 1958
(courtesy USO)

to tell him. 'Hey, the Chinese have come across.' He said, 'You're kiddin"!' I said, 'No, I'm not kidding, Bob, that's not a joking matter. We could have been killed.' As usual, Bob laughed. He's number one to me—a Prince. "And, take note, we have never had a written contract between us all those years."

"I love and will always appreciate my friend Les Brown. Once, when we were headed for Iceland, I learned that a second plane had to turn back to Prestwick to pickup a drummer from Les' band who had dallied too long in the snack bar. After the plane was back in the air again, the drummer remembered the sax player wasn't on board, so the plane had to turn back and make a second landing. The pilot insisted that another nose count be made before the plane took off again. 'That won't be necessary, Bob, 'Les said, 'Get out your instruments fellers, and strike a chord. I'll know then if anyone is missing.'

"Les Brown's band handled the laundry problem with their usual aplomb. They ignored it. One NBC executive who went with us on the tour still wears the Purple Heart we awarded him for being aboard the band's plane the day its air conditioning conked out."

Bob and I traveled all over the world to entertain our guys and gals in uniform. It was the real thing. Over the years people stop me and want to thank us for being there with Bob Hope, making their lives, during those tough times, a little happier. We did a lot of stateside shows at all the big places during the war. We did many a free concert at nearby camps wherever we traveled. Sometimes we would stop off at a camp or installation and do an impromptu show for servicemen; then we'd go on to our next regular stop...like the Meadowbrook in New Jersey or the Cafe Rouge in the Pennsylvania Hotel in New York, and other places too. I loved working with Bob. He is a true patriot.

Bob and I began our association in 1947, as a backup band for his NBC radio show and continued into the 1990s including our work together on 18 Christmas tours overseas.

A statement from Bob about the recent death of Les Brown:

"The world has lost a great musician. I have lost my music man, my sideman, my straight man, and a special friend."

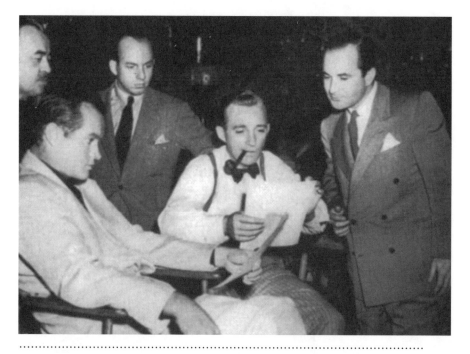

On the Road to Zanzibar set Bob, Bing, songwriters Jimmy VanHeusen and Johnny Burke check details *(courtesy Paramount Pictures)*

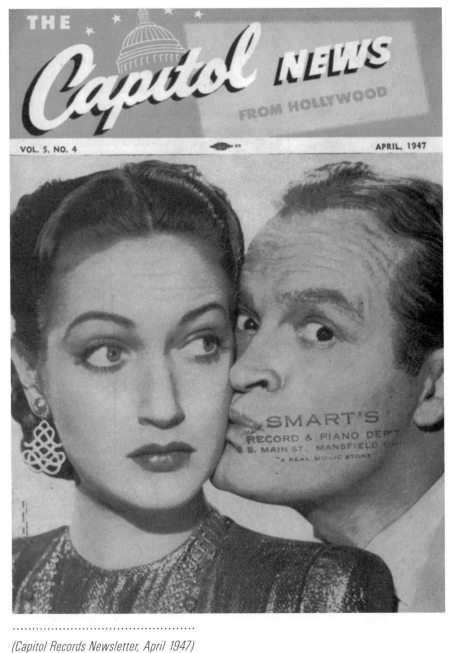

THE

Capitol NEWS

FROM HOLLYWOOD

VOL. 5, NO. 4   APRIL, 1947

(Capitol Records Newsletter, April 1947)

★★★★★★★★★★★★★★★★★★★★★★★★★★★★★

ACT SIX:
TRIBUTES FROM FRIENDS

PERSONAL GLIMPSES—IN THEIR OWN WORDS

Introduction: John Steinbeck

New York Herald Tribune, London. July 20, 1943

Random gleanings

When the time for recognition of service to the nation in wartime comes to be considered, Bob Hope should be high on the list. This man drives himself and is driven. It is impossible to see how he can do so much, can cover so much ground, can work so hard and can be so effective. He has caught the soldier's imagination. His wit is topical, both broad and caustic, but it is never aimed at people, but at conditions and ideas.

He provides laughter for men who needed it.

At Hospitals:

It hurts many of the men to laugh. It hurts their bones, it strains their sutured incisions, yet their laughter is a great medicine.

He does four sometimes five shows a day.

He builds new shows constantly. He never rests. His energy is boundless.

He takes his shows all over, not only to the big camps. They always know in advance when he is coming. It would be a terrible thing if he never showed up. He always shows up.

He walks into the aisles between the beds and says, seriously: Fellows, the folks at home are having a terrible time about eggs. They can't find any powdered eggs at all. They've got to use the old-fashioned kind you break open."

There is a man for you...There is *really* a man.

Charlton Heston
BEVERLY HILLS, CA., JUNE 2001

I've shared, with most of the rest of the world, Bob Hope's extraordinary gifts over the last four generations. Though I never had the pleasure of working with Bob, I admire not only his enormous skills as an entertainer but also the countless visits he made to our troops through three wars. I ran into Bob in Vietnam where he'd taken his fabulous troupe and where I was about to get on a helicopter to tour the Montnyard country in isolated areas where a troupe as large as Bob's couldn't conceivably go. We chatted for a moment then Bob said, "Gee, Chuck, if you could only sing I'd give you a job."

Bob Hope is surely one of the icons of entertainment in the Twentieth Century. A true American Treasure.

(courtesy Movie Star News)

RHONDA FLEMING
LOS ANGELES, CALIFORNIA, JULY 2001

I am truly happy about the publication of this tribute to Bob Hope.

I was fortunate to have made two films with my friend Bob—*The Great Lover* in 1949, which happened when I was making *A Connecticut Yankee in King Arthur's Court* with Bing Crosby. Bob came on the set one afternoon and after hanging around the set for a while, said to Bing, "Well, if you can use her—I can too." So he hired me for *The Great Lover*. Then I appeared in Bob's movie *Alias Jesse James* in 1959, where I play Jesse James' girlfriend. Bob had me appear on several

Bob Hope television specials, one with Jane Russell which also featured Bob's other leading ladies. One of my biggest regrets occurred when Bob personally telephoned me at Christmas time to go with him overseas to entertain the troops, something I had always wanted to do. I had just finished a show in Las Vegas and had gowns and scores ready, but there was a large family gathering planned for that Christmas, a gathering I was totally committed to, so I sadly declined. Bob was deeply disappointed, as no one had ever turned him down before and he didn't quite understand. I realized I missed a great opportunity. However, I did tour military hospitals and bases later, and also flew to Panama where I performed and sang for our service men and women.

In one of his biographies, Bob wrote that the two classiest women he knew were his wife, Dolores, and myself—the high-

Bob Hope and
Rhonda
Fleming, who
plays Jesse
James' girl
friend, in a
farewell that is
interrupted and
never comes off
in "Alias Jesse
James," *(cour-
tesy United
Artists)*

est of compliments—I was happy to receive from Bob. Dolores has been a great wife and keeps him going. What a life and legacy!

Bob was known to rehearse a lot— quite the opposite of Bing Crosby. Bob had very well planned scenes and happy, busy sets. He was great to work with, but I often wondered how they did all the *Road* pictures together with their opposite styles of rehearsals.

I must say that I am delighted to be a part of this wonderful tribute to Bob. He really deserves all the best from all of us for the great deeds he has accomplished in his lifetime.

PATTY ANDREWS
NORTHRIDGE, CALIFORNIA, JUNE 2001

Patty is, of course, one third of the great girl singing group of World War II and beyond, The Andrews Sisters, and has worked alongside Bob Hope many, many times. Bob always admired the girls, Patty, Maxene & La Verne, and invited them often to appear on his radio, and later, TV shows, as well as their participation in one of the *Road* pictures where the girls sang with Bing Crosby in a few sketches. The girls are best known for their wonderful recordings "Bei Mir Bist Dunking Schon," "I'll Be with You in Apple Blossom Time," "Rum and Coca Cola," "Don't Sit Under the Apple Tree," "Pistol Packin' Momma," and "Don't Fence Me In," with Bing Crosby; and, in the movie *Road to Rio* with Bob Hope and Bing Crosby, they sang "You Don't Have to Know the Language," and "Apalachicola, FLA." with Bing.

Patty Andrews
(R. Grudens collection)

Everybody loves Bob Hope. You know, we Andrews Sisters did a lot of stateside USO shows with him during the war, especially at hospitals and army bases.

I'll never forget one time at what is now the LA airport—it used to be a marsh—where we were picked up by an army plane to go to different places where we performed. On the way back—we were coming home late at night—we thought we were going direct to LA, but, and you know how BIG Bob was at the time—they actually landed the plane in Palm Springs almost up to Bob's front porch. How BIG is that?

We also did shows down in Palm Springs, and after the show we were invited up to the big round house he had. Everybody attended. It was heaven for us girls.

Bob is amazing. At his age today—actually not too many months ago—he was on a show we did with Les Brown—a celebration of Les' birthday, and Bob and Dolores came on. Bob had to be helped on stage and Dolores was center at the mike. Bob stood next to her. She turned to him and she says, "Bob, why don't you sing that song you used to do in the act?" Bob replied, "Oh, you mean 'Thanks for the Memory,' and she said yes, and he said OK. Now, at this time Bob was almost blind and very hard of hearing—he in the high nineties, you know. Well, he sang the song and many sets of lyrics, remembering every word without stumbling. He's remarkable. He is always full of life. When I think about the years he used to do the Academy Award shows—he did them for over 14 years. He was always so fast. Nobody could ever replace him.

And Bob was always good to everybody, Richard, everybody! And he was never mean or disrespectful to his fellow performers or other workers on the set. With his money, he doesn't have to be anything but nice. (laughs)

I remember when Bob, Bing, Dottie Lamour and us girls made one of the Road pictures—the *Road to Rio*. On the set the boys each had their own writers. One would try to top the other and that went on for the entire picture. They would never stick to the script. They would break each other up and everybody on the set. Dottie Lamour would scream at them. The scene would supposed to last a certain time, you know, and being impatient to do her part, she would shout to them, "Break it up fellows! Come on—cut it out. I want to go home. Stop it, for God's sake."

We girls befriended Dottie during the filming and we all embarked on a personal appearance tour with Bing and Bob to promote the film. What fun that was for everyone.

With Bob Hope it was good times, good laughs, always. Bob is truly one of a kind. And Dolores, she really sings up a storm. People listen and cry when she sings some of her special songs, "It's Only a Paper Moon," or "Silent Night." Bob and Dolores Hope are just very amazing.

PAT BOONE
BEVERLY HILLS, CALIFORNIA, JUNE 2001

Bob Hope has always been wonderful to me, supportive and encouraging and aware that I too have a sense of humor. Between us we have a mutual admiration society going with more more admiration on my side of the equation.

We have had many memorable, funny interludes together on golf courses and elsewhere. I recall once when Bing Crosby, Bob and I were having lunch together in the NBC commissary. Bing, Bob and I had already ordered when bandleader, comedian Phil Harris suddenly rushes up and says: "Hey guys, let's ditch this place. Right down the street there's a topless bowling alley! Let's go there."

Bing, even before Bob could think of a rejoinder, from being startled, looked up and quietly said, "Oh sure! Just what we need—a couple of sweaty paps in our face while we're trying to eat lunch."

Well, that ended that!

A young Pat Boone *(courtesy Movie Star News)*

Some years ago when I had to close a big celebrity show after a major golf amateur tournament in Ohio, I didn't want to follow Bob Hope on stage (you'd have to be an idiot), but Bob had booked yet another appearance somewhere else after our evening event in Columbus. He had a plane standing by to whisk him to his next event and was in a hurry to do his part of the show and let me finish—a spot I wouldn't leave to a leopard.

Though it was his idea, he instinctively wanted to do a show that would make anything that came after it anticlimactic, and he pulled out all the stops.

He joked, he sang, he danced, he wowed the audience and left them standing, begging for more, as I waited hopelessly, sweating in the wings.

As he came off, and my musicians tried to quickly set up for my introduction, I asked him, "Bob, tell me, you got a standing ovation when you went on; you got another when you came off; and now they're standing after your encore—wanting even more. What does that feel like?"

Bob lowered his head slightly, looked up at me with that cockeyed leer on his face and drawled, "You'll never know....."

And I never have.

ROSEMARY CLOONEY

BEVERLY HILLS, CALIFORNIA, JUNE 2001

Bob Hope's humor is nonpartisan and always topical. Sure, he talks a lot about politics in his monologues, that's part of his schtick. Anyone who has spent time working with Bob Hope has a little bit of his luster rub off on them. And that doesn't get past many politicians; as they would like very much to have some of the acceptance that Bob has received from all over the world, thanks to his millions of miles traveled for the USO entertaining our guys and gals, one of the most important things in Bob's life.

One of Bob's secrets is his ability to sleep the moment he sets his mind to it. So there's no time wasted. Those cat naps help him tremendously—over all other performers. He is never tired.

And, I was with Kathryn Crosby, Bob Hope and Phil Harris when Bing Crosby was laid to rest in Hollywood. We both shared that sad and very poignant day with and for a true friend whom we both loved dearly and will always miss.

ANN JILLIAN

WOODLAND HILLS, CALIFORNIA, JULY 2001

THE SCENE: IN THE WAR ZONE OFF BEIRUT, LEBANON; CHRISTMAS 1983.

Ann shares her memory of an unforgettable tour with Bob Hope

He sits, hands folded, chin tucked into his collar, eyelids peacefully closed to the scene outside, even though he's such a central part of it. Here's Bob Hope, for decades our *Mr.*

America, our goodwill ambassador, resting peacefully on a crate of ammunition in a *Foxfire* boat, not far from the machine guns mounted at either end of this mini war vessel.

Two Navy Seals man these ominous looking weapons, but he's blissfully calm enough to pay no attention. I am enthralled with this picture of opposites— an old man in his 80s seemingly unconcerned with the volatile setting where mostly the young and strong survive. Meanwhile the young and strong among us are shivering.

We're told we're past curfew. That means no lights are allowed. That also means we couldn't fly back to the aircraft carrier that's been serving as our USO "hotel." Instead, we're slipping back to the carrier in a *Foxfire* gunboat...without lights. We're only a mile off shore and the enemy tends to fire at anything that moves on the water. Should the boat capsize, we're instructed not to "cry out," "Don't worry," they say; they'll find us. (Yeah, but in what condition?)

I swallow. Hard. My heart pounds. Even the exciting prospect of being rescued at sea by these virile young men doesn't help. Panic strikes my heart when I think of the *nasty* things swimming around in these waters, nipping at my appendages and various other body parts. I search the face of my husband, Andy, and I can see he's worried, too.

We look at each other and then all eyes turn to the tranquil *Old Man of the Sea*. Framed by the wake stirred up by the boat, doused by an eerie red glow, he naps the revitalizing naps he's famous for taking anywhere, anytime. Clearly, he's done this all before—and that has a comforting effect on all of us. He has a mission: to bring laughs to men; to bring the warmth of home to these sons and daughters so far away from their families and friends.

Suddenly, a massive, brightly-lit wall of metal rises out of the sea and an iron monolith towers over us. It's our destination, our hotel on the sea, the U.S.S. Guam.

There's a tiny, unsteady dock for us to *hop* onto. If we time the rhythm of our *hops* wrong, we'll be smashed like squid being pounded by peasant fishermen. And it just keeps getting better. I spy a chain ladder hanging down the side of this monstrous ship. Was that lowered to receive us? How many stories do we have to go up? But our father figure isn't napping now. He stands confidently, with his ever-present masseuse at his side, and hops the bouncing boat to the dock without missing a beat. The chain ladder? He did that too!

O.K., now it's our turn. We followed him, like children marching behind the Pied Piper. We were the troupe of performers for the Christmas of 1983, chosen by Bob Hope to entertain our peacekeeping troops off the shores of Beirut, Lebanon. It was the world's hot-spot.

Today, so many years later, the memory plays back in my mind as vividly as if I were standing there again breathing in the salt air blowing off the coast of Lebanon. It's just one of many amazing memories I've had the privilege of sharing with Bob Hope and his lovely wife, Dolores.

Though I'd been a performer since childhood, it was my humble opinion that you just weren't officially in show business until you had been asked to perform with Bob Hope and the USO for our troops. So when my phone rang, and I got the invitation, I was thrilled as a person has a right to be!

"Look Ma, I made it! Top of the world!" I wanted to shout, just like Jimmy Cagney did in the fiery climax of *White Heat*. Of course, time soon taught me the true treasures of the trip. They're the same treasures that Bob discovered long ago. They are revealed in his eyes when he looks at all of them, the men and women laughing at his skits or standup, whistling and grunting in good-humored appreciation of the performers he brought with him, or, in almost reverential silence when a poignant ballad is sung, heads are bowed and eyes are wiped dry.

I spied such a moment when we performed that night. Bob's eyes filled with tears, glistening in the reflection of the television lights as he watched them take the show in with such joy. Slightly startled at my intrusion, he quietly nodded, "They're my guys and gals," then gave me a humble smile. There was a treasure to hold onto. I'll never forget it.

Nor will I ever forget the encouragement he gave so freely. "You sure put that over, Ann," he told me. "You got a lot of vaudeville in ya. They loved it!"

And another time, just before we left for Riyadh during the last weeks of Operation Desert Shield: "Hey, Ann," he asked, "How 'bout singing that song you sang last time in Beirut, 'Wind Beneath My Wings?' That was a big hit!" I might add, with great pride, that I introduced that song on television in the Beirut Special. Composer Larry Henley very graciously told me so in a letter of thanks. Bob Hope's enthusiastic support of all my efforts will be gratefully held forever in my heart.

In April of 1985, after the news of my fight with breast cancer had broken, I found myself inundated with a sea of flowers and well wishes from so many friends, in and out of my profession. But I still remember the arrival of the granddaddy of all floral arrangements at my hospital room: An ENORMOUS profusion of white roses and flowers with a card urging me to, ...Hurry up and get out of there; they're playing our cue! Signed, Bob Hope. The whole floor was abuzz.

To speak of Bob Hope and not to recall memorable moments with Dolores would be highly remiss. Dolores Hope and I spent hours playing *song* games on the way to Saudi Arabia. We kept at it, I'll admit, until the eyes of all the guys, even my husband's, were crossed. We had a wonderful time. Listening to her beautiful voice was a delight. We shared oodles of 'girl talk' because Dolores and I and their daughter, Linda, who was the producer of the show, were the only females of our entourage allowed to enter Riyadh. We have shopped together in military bases around the world, giggled and reminisced, and I hold those times as very dear.

Even my little son, Andy, has been touched by their thoughtfulness. He, too, will have his own set of special memories.

This is the Bob Hope that I know, the heart that I saw, the enthusiasm and compassion that I witnessed up close. It's my specialsal view of the Mr. America thousands eagerly awaited to view.

I am thankful to you Bob. Thank you for the chance to be *officially* a part of show biz. Thank you for the chance to work with you in front of the camera and on the road, to share in the awesome thrill of being with you in this nation's ticker tape parade for our forces returning home from Desert Storm.

As so many have said before, Bob, Thanks for the Memories.

TONY BENNETT

In 1984, during an interview with Tony Bennett at Westbury Music Fair, Tony told me about his first encounter with Bob Hope, the man who chaned Tony's then stage name of Joe Bari, to Tony Bennett, based on his real name Anthony Dominick Benedetto on the very day he was invited by Bob to appear with him and Pearl Bailey spotted Tony signing in Greenwich Village at the Village Barn on West 8th Street and alerted Bob who visited him there the next evening:

When I was at the front in Germany during World War II, I was privileged to attend one of Bob Hope's GI shows. He was there with Jane Russell, Jerry Colonna, and Les Brown's band. It was terrific. One of the best things that ever happened to me — it boosted mine and thousands of others' morale when we really needed it. Bob is the reason I decided to go into this business. He made me realize a laugh or a song made people happy. It was like Bob Hope had saved all our lives. And, it wasn't the last time he saved mine. All the GI's loved him, believe me. I was there.

(Tony Bennett collection)

Anybody that ever did anything for Bob Hope was repaid tenfold. It was an honor appearing later with Bob at the Paramount. I could hardly believe my good luck. When I finished my first number Bob said to the audience: "Well, I was getting tired of Crosby anyhow." It helped me win the audienc, who enjoyed the usual Crosby barb delivered by Bob, although, of course, I was no match for Bing, one of my early mentors. We went on a six city tour that ended in California. There, Bob introduced me to Bing, one of the great thrills of my life. Everywhere Bob Hope traveled, people went crazy. They still do.

JAMES BACON, *Noted Author and Columnist*
NORTHRIDGE, CALIFORNIA, JULY 2001

I've traveled the world with Bob Hope—from Alaska to Vietnam. Invariably, on all these trips, especially among the U.S. troops in Vietnam, some young guy would walk right past Bob Hope to accost me. His typical comment would be: "Mr. Bacon, my mother went to high school with you at Lock Haven, (Pa.) high school.

This happened so many times that it became a running gag with Hope. He once accused me of paying those guys to pull the Lock Haven bit. Once at his golf tournament in London, he even put Lock Haven and me in his monologue.

I never bribed anyone. Over some twenty years of traveling with Hope, it must have happened a couple hundred times.

Then in 1978, I got an invitation to the White House from President Jimmy Carter. The occasion was a reception for Hope's 75th birthday. It also was the chance for me to pull the ultimate Lock Haven gag in reverse.

All guests went through a receiving line, greeting the President first and then Hope who was standing next to him. As I shook hands with President Carter, I told him: Mr. President, I'm from Lock Haven, Pa. At that the President grabbed me by the shoulder and with that famous Carter smile said: "That's my favorite town in the U.S. outside of Plains, Georgia." He was enthusiastic in his praise of my home town.

Hope next grabbed me by the shoulder and practically screamed: "You

James Bacon
(courtesy NBC)

wouldn't dare set up the President of the United States with the Lock Haven gag, would you?"

Carter was a little taken back at first by Hope's remarks but managed to ask: "How's my church? Is it still functioning?"

I told him it was. Then I explained to Hope something I had never told him before. Jimmy Carter, long before he entered politics, was a missionary for the Southern Baptist church. His first stop was Lock Haven where he founded a Southern Baptist church which, as far as I know, is still there. At least it was the last time I visited my home town a couple of years ago.

Carter had the last word before the dumbfounded Hope could speak again.

"The congregation was so small, I invited all of them to my inauguration."

Another amusing incident with Hope happened on the last Christmas show in 1972. The troupe always stayed in Bangkok ever since the Viet Cong a year or so earlier had blown up the Bachelor Officers Quarters where we were supposed to stay in Saigon. Some 43 or 44 officers were killed in the blast which the Hope troupe missed by a half hour. The reason we were late was because Barney McNulty, Hope's long-time cue card guy, was a half hour late catching the plane in Bangkok.

"I refuse to leave without my ad lib's," quipped Hope while waiting for Barney who was always late. Barney died last year and even his funeral service was a half hour late in starting.

But his tardiness in Bangkok was a Godsend. This a roundabout way of getting to the punch line of this story.

As you probably know, Dolores Hope is a devout Catholic. Hope is not. He was born Anglican in a London suburb. His father, a skilled stone mason, emigrated to America and his first job was helping to build the Euclid Avenue Presbyterian Church in Cleveland, Ohio.

In a few years the father brought over Bob and the rest of the family. "When we all saw that beautiful church my father worked on, we became Presbyterians on the spot," Hope recalled.

But this particular Christmas Eve in Bangkok, Bob and I were in an Air Force Catholic chapel for midnight mass. He traditionally attended midnight mass every Christmas as a favor to Dolores.

We had just returned from Da Nang, the airport for Saigon, where Bob and his troupe had put on a three hour show for the troops. He was tired after the long day and flight back and soon dozed off in his pew. The priest who celebrated the mass had no way of knowing that Hope was in his congregation. For the priest's sermon, he told the story of The nativity...." Joseph knocked on the door of the inn," the priest intoned, "but when the door opened..." .....the priest paused in open mouth surprise because he had just spotted the sleeping Hope. From the pulpit, he literally yelled: "BOB HOPE! BOB HOPE!"

The yell woke up Hope who turned to me and said: "What did I do?"

FRANKIE LAINE
SAN DIEGO, CALIFORNIA, JUNE 2001

Frankie Laine has worked with Bob Hope many times. With a string of great hit records that includes "Jezebel," "That's My Desire," his own composition "We'll Be Together Again," "Lucky Old Sun," "I Believe," and "Shine," among many others, Frank is still singing at the age of eighty-six, having just performed in Las Vegas. He talks about Bob Hope, a man he fiercely admires:

With Bob, back in the 1940s, I did an army USO show at March Air Force Base, also at Barstow, and we worked a show together on a gigantic battleship in Long Beach. That was something. He handled an audience perfectly. Those boys were in the palm of his hand. He knew just what they wanted to hear. He'd memorize the names of local commanders and used them in his patter, to the delight of everyone. They would roar. Bob was always at home in radio, television, on stage, even on a battleship. He proved all of that.

In 1948 and 9 we did a radio show together, and in 1954 we both entertained in London at a Command Performance. We stood side by side as Queen Elizabeth herself shook hands with about twelve of us performers. It was a proud moment.

Bob, Joan
Davis and
Frankie Laine
(courtesy
F. Laine
collection)

With a little effort I managed to jockey myself into the right position for an impending photograph, thanks to advise from the photographer whom I knew. Singer Guy Mitchell was on my right and Bob on my left along with author, playwright Noel Coward, on his left.

Bob and I got lucky, as the photo chosen by the world's media was plastered on the face of every newspaper in the world and we were smack in the middle of it. The photo was used for a later album cover.

It was also in 1954 that Bob, the beautiful actress Hedy Lamarr, and I performed at the North Island Naval Air Station in San Diego, near where I now live. Some show! Bob was always in enthusiastic, rare form.

In 1950 Bob and I, with Louis Armstrong, Jerry Lewis and Dean Martin, and Deborah Kerr appeared on Tallulah Bankhead's *Big Show Broadcast*, radio's last stand against television, live at the old Center Theater in Rockefeller Center on the corner of 49th and Sixth Avenue. Ironically, Richard Grudens, our author here, was a studio page for NBC and worked on the same show. (The theater in now gone.)

I have also worked on some of Bob's charity shows in Palm Springs, and we spent a lot of time together at the Desert Inn in Las Vegas during a week-long golf outing called the *Tournament of Champions*. That's when we got to know one another. Bob loved the way I did some of those western tunes like "Mule Train," "Rawhide," and the song theme to "Gunfight At the OK Corral," and "High Noon." Everyone we met during that time held a special feeling for him. He would brag to everyone about me. You could tell each time he encountered someone that he knew or had worked with, the magic was always present. It was an aura—something special.

Once, I shared a table at dinner with Bob and New York Daily Mirror columnist, powerful Walter Winchell. Listening to Bob work his wonders with the man taught me a lot of lessons of presence. It is just great knowing Bob Hope and being able to call him my friend.

I think he feels the same way.

FRANCES LANGFORD
JENSEN BEACH, FLORIDA, JULY 2001

When Bob and I first decided to go to Alaska, my husband, actor Jon Hall was against it because he thought I had symptoms of acute appendicitis. "You can't go," he said to me, and

....
The Original Crew. Bob, Frances Langford, Tony Romano, Jerry Colonna at P-38 Base, North Africa 1943 *(courtesy USO)*
....

I said to him," They have doctors in Alaska, too." End of argument.

Traveling with Bob and the troupe was the best experience of my show business life.

Once, when we were traveling in a storm on the way to Anchorage, the pilots were arguing, and that worried Bob and I. We had been circling through the storm for forty-five minutes. Bob nicknamed the pilots Junior and Growing Pains because they were just twenty-one and twenty-two. The mechanic came back and told us to put our parachutes on, and, in case we landed in the water, a Mae West too. We'd heard that the water was so cold up here that you lived only forty-five seconds in it. Bob couldn't say any funny lines because his teeth was chattering. Then the sun broke out and we landed safely.

People have said that they could not get on another plane after an experience like that. I know that Doris Day was affected that way after many, many flights with Bob. I couldn't sleep that night. Little did we know that the army had every anti-aircraft searchlight searching for us—all thirty of them. They were worried because the pilot had gone off beam and we were lost. The pilot found one of the the beams, and even with the radio out, followed it down and landed safely. Bob and I have logged a million miles since flying on the USO trips.

SALLY BENNETT
PALM BEACH, FLORIDA, AUGUST 10, 2001

Big Band enthusiast Sally Bennett has done it all, including giving birth to the Big Band Hall of Fame and Museum. Also from Cleveland, Ohio, Sally and Bob Hope have crossed paths many times. Bob has been a longtime member of the Honorary Board which also includes Donald Trump, George Hamilton, Joe Franklin, and Merv Griffin. The Big Band Hall of Fame & Museum, located in West Palm Beach, Florida, finally came to fruition just a few years ago, and has recently installed Frances Langford, Tommy Dorsey bandleader Buddy Morrow, singers Joni James, Harry Connick, Jr., Pat Boone, Don Cornell, and Glenn Miller Orchestra leader Larry O'Brien.

I treasure my long-standing association with Bob Hope, which began in the 1960s. He, of course, is a member of the Big Band Hall of Fame's Honorary Board, a result of my appearance with him in Cleveland's Cain Park where we both sang "I Wanna Man from the Moon," my own composition.

During rehearsal time I told him of my passion trying to establish the Big Band Hall of Fame, and he only encouraged me, going so far as joining up, lending his name and donating his time.

Sally Bennett and friend at Cain Park, Cleveland, Ohio *(Sally Bennett collection)*

We all know Bob always had time for everything and everyone, especially when they needed help. Bob was also a friend of my husband Paul's family.

Luckily, once again, Bob and I performed on *The Bob Hope Show* on *Cleveland Day* at the Ohio State Fair, where I sang my song "Cleveland Our Town," featured in my first book "Sugar & Spice," and as well in my second book "Magic Moments." More fond memories.

For some forty years we have kept in touch through letters, telegrams, and calls. Paul and I have exchanged Christmas Cards with Bob and Dolores without interruption all those years. For some nostalgic reason, I have kept every card.

Through all this, Bob Hope has been a tremendous influence and special part of my life in the past, present, and I hope, a long future.

I'll stay in touch, Bob. It's become a habit I'll never break.

SHIRLEY JONES
BEVERLY HILLS, CALIFORNIA, JULY 2001

Shirley Jones, happily married to comedian Marty Engels, is best known for her role as the television sit-com mom on *The Partridge Family*. Shirley's lead performances opposite

Gordon Mac Rae in two classic Rodgers and Hammerstein musical films, *Oklahoma* in 1955, her debut film, and *Carousel* in 1956, remain superlative, her loveliness and perfect interpretations of all those beautiful songs set a high standard of excellence in film musicals. Shirley won an Academy Award for her acting role in *Elmer Gantry*.

Shirley Jones and Marty Engels at home, 1988 *(courtesy Movie Star News)*

I have known Bob Hope for many years—appeared with him many times- and I think I can safely defy anyone to tell you just exactly who and what the man behind the snappy crack is. God knows, there must BE one. And he has systematically built that sardonic, self-effacing crackle into a monumental American Icon Image that far surpasses the man or his deeds. He can do no wrong. And, even when some of his wanderings hit the presses, the whole affair fades in a sea of indifference like last week's weather. He is beyond Teflon. He is *Mt. Rushmore*. So then, how can there NOT be a thinking, planning, analyzing, ambition machine somewhere in there under all that snappy patter grinding out moves and strategies and industry maneuvers of the sort that Icon Images are made??

Well, there isn't, plain and simple—not by MY observations and not by anyone's that I've ever known.

As for all my years of proximity, one incident stays with me. I put it at 1976. Bob was 73 (and very much the billionaire, even back then, no matter what the magazines estimated). I was asked to join Bob on his big Christmas Special which was to film in Montreal, Canada. Also on the special was a young comic who was taking the country by storm, Freddie Prinze.

We did the show—huge, live audience—I was waiting at the front door with Freddie (who was absolutely beside himself to be working with Bob.) He had done the show, opened for Bob, but had not yet met him. Suddenly the big black car made its turn and it was upon us. The door opened and it was The Hope himself waving us on in; I got in and then turned to see a rather shaky footed Freddie negotiating his way down into the long limo that would drive away with him sitting smack next to the world's most famous living comedian. And there we were—the three of us—Caesar Chavez, Snow White and John D. Rockefeller; And what were the first words from this absurd triumvirate? I'll tell you what they were. And maybe they'll give you an insight as to our very private icon's priorities.

Jones: "So, where do we go to eat?"
Prinze: "My family is with me at the hotel. I know my mom would be thrilled to meet you both."
The Great White Hope: "I just don't why I can't get that Hollywood closer bit to work. It slays 'em on the tube. You saw it Freddie—do you think I'd be better off taking it out or moving it up closer to my opening?"
Your call.
Marty Engels: "I love it, Shirley. Just love it!"

CONNIE HAINES
CLEARWATER, FLORIDA, JULY 2001

Where do I begin when recalling all the wonderful moments I spent with my dear friend and fellow performer, Bob Hope. Well, I first met Bob right after leaving Frank Sinatra and the Tommy Dorsey Orchestra in the early forties. I was twenty-one and Bob was almost forty.

Bob had asked me to appear with him on his radio show and in the USO shows for the Armed Forces. What a thrill it was for a young singer like me. It was during the filming of a *Road* picture with Bing Crosby. As you know Bob and Bing always played pranks on one- another.

On one particular radio show we did during the war called *Command Performances*, the script called for Bing, Frank Sinatra, and Bob himself to be bickering over who would take me to dinner after the show. Of course, in reality we all went

"Les Girls", Jane
Russell, Connie
Haines, and
Beryl Davis
*(Connie Haines
collection)*

to dinner together after the show and enjoyed a great time and more laughs than you could count. It was truly a memorable show. What a time to be in show business and work with all the greats.

Bob always helped advance my career, asking me to perform on his tours, giving me full support, never trying to take the show away from me like many other comics. Bob is down to earth and always interested in his co-stars. He would always insist I complete my full show, a big grin on his face shines when I would receive a standing ovation. I felt special when performing with him. He never realized how famous he was then. In those days we would end the show with a chorus of "It's De-Lovely" and close with "Thanks for the Memory," a cherished moment always.

I sang with Bob Hope many times throughout my career, the last time about ten years ago when he came to Florida, and called me from the airport and asked me to join him in a charity show supporting his favorite "Parkinson's Disease Charity." Bob has slowed down so our paths do not cross like the old days. I will always remember my kind, generous, wonderful friend, Bob Hope, whom I love.

BERYL DAVIS
PALM SPRINGS, CALIFORNIA, JULY 2001

Beryl Davis and friends on the Paramount set, 1940s *(Beryl Davis collection)*

I've had a terrific association with Bob Hope, and it began before I ever met him. My father headed up a big band in England, so I began singing as a teenager with his band and later with musicians Stephane Grappelli and Django Reinhardt in Paris. In England, I sang with the Glenn Miller Army Air Force Band, and was the last singer to perform with Glenn before his tragic disappearance. I actually wore an air force style uniform while performing.

Word came from Bob Hope in America that he was interested in hiring me to sing on his radio show in Los Angeles. His agent approached me through Tutti Camaretta, a musician and arranger with Tommy Dorsey, and Willard Alexander, who headed a big band agency that represented Glenn Miller and other big bands of the day.

To me it was a miracle. I signed for six shows with Bob. Willard brought me to New York and had me sing with Vaughn Monroe's band at the Strand Theater on Broadway as sort of a

tryout. I took a train to LA and hooked up with Bob Hope and we went to Ontario, Canada for my first performance. This was in 1947.

Bob thought, because I was an Englishwoman, that I would have a thick accent, but I didn't. I had emulated all the American singers so I practiced speaking that American way, so I didn't have much of an accent, so Bob said: "Could you do your bit more British like?" Guess he wanted a British accent he could bounce off.

Bob was always very kind to me. When I was green and knew nothing about Hollywood, Bob and his wife, Dolores, helped me at every turn.

Later, when I was married to disc jockey Peter Potter, we were having a child, and one day received a call from Bob asking us if he could use the name Peter Potter for a movie he was making with a friend of mine, Jane Russell. The movie was *The Paleface.* In the opening scene Jane was sitting on a mountain and Bob was in a covered wagon that had a sign that read "Painless Peter Potter, Dentist."

Of course, we happily gave Bob permission. The contract said he would pay us one dollar. We were excited to do something for Bob, after all, it was Bob who brought me to America.

Again—a bit later, Bob helped Jane Russell, Connie Haines, and myself promote our singing act, "Les Girls" by allowing us to appear on his show many times. He did everything he could do to help us. If we had a special charity project and needed to promote it, Bob was there to help always. Nobody could do more. He would have us at his golf tournaments and visit us at our performances. He was always intwined in my life. He made my life in America possible. Here I am now sitting in this beautiful place, thanks to Bob. Remember too that Bob and I both come from jolly old England.

To me, Bob Hope represents all good and positive things in my life. God bless him and Dolores for all they do for so many.

DORIS DAY

CARMEL, CALIFORNIA, JUNE 2001

Bob feels that Doris Day is one of the great singers, and rates her along with Judy Garland as a great performer, and one of his favorite people. He like her very much and called her J.B. (Jut-Butt). Bob would say, "You know, J.B., we could play a nice game of bridge on your butt. She was wonderful taking my kidding like that."

In between my first and second pictures at Warners, I put in a couple of tours as a member of Bob Hope's concert troupe. It was sometimes a frightening, educational, exhausting, and enjoyable experience.

Over a six week period, we traveled by a DC-6 to a different city every night—and sometimes a matinee was fitted in. It was the winter of 1948 and we flew through storms and turbulence that had me praying. We make landings where I couldn't see the airfield. There were always mobs of people greeting Bob. The crowds displaced me, but I learned to get out of the way. I also became fearful of flying.

Bob is the undisputed master of timing and delivery which are the very essence of comedy. We were very good together. There is something rewarding about generating laughs from a live audience. Bob always radiated good cheer. He was a joyous man to be around. He is very funny on his own, his mischievous face, the way his teeth take over his face when he smiles. Just watching him work makes you feel good. Some people say that about me, which makes me happy to hear.

When the tour ended, we did a weekly radio show out of Hollywood. I would sing a song, usually a ballad like "It's Magic," and then Bob and I would play a sketch. It was Bob's comedy skill and it was the eagerness of the studio audience to laugh that brought the mediocre skits off, as most of the time they were only slightly funny.

Those shows taught me a lot of interesting lessons about how to run my own career, and how to listen to my own inner voice instead of relying on false superlatives for reassurance.

Working with Bob Hope was an invigorating experience to say the least.

MARGARET WHITING
NEW YORK, NEW YORK, JULY 2001

Margaret Whiting has spent her life singing beautiful songs, making records of those songs, and performing them just about everywhere. Her dad, Richard Whiting, a legendary songwriter, composed the great standards "Japanese Sandman," "My Ideal," and "Till We Meet Again." When Margaret was growing up, regular visitors to her home included Eddie Cantor, Al Jolson, Johnny Mercer, Jerome Kern and George Gershwin, to name a few. Margaret was taken under Johnny Mercer's wing when her dad passed on. Under Johnny's guidance at Capitol Records, Margaret's first hit was "That Old Black Magic." Besides working with Bob, Margaret toured with *4 Girls 4*, with Helen O'Connell, Fran Warren, and Kay Starr.

Of course, I was very close to Bob Hope working with him at least two days and two nights every week for seven years as the featured singer on his radio show. Even during the very focused time of rewriting next week's radio script to fit whomever would be starring with him, he would be there with his usual laugh, making jokes and seeing that everyone at rehearsal was comfortable and making us all feel very much at home. His rehearsals were hilarious, with announcer Bill Goodwin and Jerry Colonna always trying to top the master with their stories— but, as always, Hope came in at the last, topping everyone.

Whenever we went on a trip we flew in a special airplane with the band and everyone on the show. Bob would walk down the aisle telling funny stories, making sure everyone was comfortable. When we entertained the armed forces, Bob always brought

Margaret Whiting with Bob and orchestra leader Billy May *(courtesy NBC)*

along glamorous women and pretty young things whom he knew the men, who were thousands of miles from home, would enjoy.

I remember most of all our holiday trip to Thule, Greenland and Goose Bay, Labrador. We flew in the President's airplane, and took along William Holden, Bill's wife, Brenda Marshall, actress/model Anita Eckberg (actually a substitute for Marilyn Monroe—who canceled) Hollywood columnist Hedda Hopper, comedian Jerry Colonna, regular Peter Leeds, dancer Patty Thomas and the entire Les Brown Band.

We were about to land, but because there were 160 mile-an-hour winds, the pilot told us we shouldn't try to land. But, Bob said, "We've come all this way to entertain the boys, so let's do it."

Unknown to Bob, the people on the ground had been standing there at least five hours in the sub-zero cold, wind, and snow, waiting for the plane to land. When we were finally ready to disembark the plane, I was right behind Bob. He suddenly stepped back into the plane with tears in his eyes seeing all those people standing there with tears in their eyes, realizing they had been literally standing there for all that time in that absolutely terrible weather. If you weren't used to it, and were not adequately protected, you could die in that weather, it was that cold. He was visibly shaken and had to pull himself together. Then, in the usual Hope style, with great warmth, he went down and greeted everyone with hugs and kisses. The Air Force band had struck up Bob's theme, "Thanks for the Memory," adding to the high emotional setting. The rest of us trooped behind him and were shown our quarters which were located underground.

The show was a terrific success, and I know that everyone watching it and all of us who gave up our holidays to go there, had the best time of our lives.

That is some of the magic of Bob Hope.

LARRY GELBART
BEVERLY HILLS, CALIFORNIA, JULY 2001

Larry Gelbart is the legendary comedy writer who created the television show "M*A*S*H," authored the Broadway

smash "Something Funny Happened on the Way to the Forum," the Broadway show "City of Angels," and the film script for "Tootsie."

An early 1950s television writer along with fellow writers Mel Brooks, Neil Simon, Carl Reiner, Woody Allen, responsible for the success of the television comedy showcase "Your Show of Shows" in the 1950s that starred Sid Caesar, Imogene Coca, Carl Reiner and Howard Morris, Larry was also a premier writer for Bob Hope.

I traveled with Bob to Tokyo in 1952 to help prepare comedy scripts. On the way we stopped off at Kwajalein, Guam and Okinawa. One night while we were driving through Tokyo, I said to Bob, 'Boy, I wish they'd start another war in Hollywood so we could go home.'

Bob said to Larry after a few days of touring Tokyo, "How about this place, Larry,' he asked. 'It's different, isn't it?"

Larry spat back: "It sure is, but everything you see is marked, 'Made in Japan.'"

"Larry is one of the best writers I ever had," says Bob. "As time went by and my radio chores became burdensome, he would submit comedy material to me as one my writers and I would edit it. The idea was for all the writers to prepare material and for me to edit it to my taste and style, although there was little editing after a while, Larry and the others understanding my need for topical material and anything current."

I liked working for Bob. I never felt exploited or put upon by him. He never would call me in the middle of the night for jokes like he did with some of his other writers. He is a funny man, no doubt, and I constantly laughed at him. With Bob it was different than working for other comedians who stay put in one place for at least a while. You were always with Bob because you were traveling with him. I went to London, Berlin, Korea, Alaska, you name it. It was a great experience writing for and traveling with Bob Hope and his crew of musicians, writers, and performers. Nothing else ever came close.

*****

Here are some Gelbart (written with others) samples written for the Korean trip

Some of these towns are changing hands so fast one soldier bought a lamp with three thousand Won (Korean money) and got his change in Rubles. ...Seoul has changed hands so many times the towels are marked, HIS, HERS, and WHO'S SORRY NOW?......I asked a GI here how to tell a North Korean from a South Korean and he said, 'Turn your back,'...and...There are no psychiatrists in Korea...........they know you're nuts or you wouldn't be here.

Larry was stirred with emotion witnessing events while writing for Bob on the Korean trip. Years later, he created the series "M*A*S*H" as a result of his experience with the Hope show in Korea.

An important writer for Broadway shows, Larry was once asked what they should do with Hitler if they captured him, and he replied," Send him on the road with a Broadway musical."

PHYLLIS DILLER
LOS ANGELES, CALIFORNIA, JULY 2001

"Bob works like hell, that's why he got where he was going. He's constantly on the go. When he hits a town, you think he'd be exhausted, but he goes out and sees if he can find people who are working—new people-and watches them."

Comedienne Phyllis Diller's entire career is aligned with Bob Hope's. She appeared in three of Bob's films: *Boy Did I Get the Wrong Number* in 1966, *Eight on the Lamb* in 1967, and *The Private Army of Sgt. O'Farrell* in 1968. Bob first

found Phyllis doing her act in a Washington, D.C. nightclub.

He had purposely come to see me because I was very new in the business and he thought I was interesting. I was working with two guys and we were bombing terribly. When I heard he was there, I tried to sneak out, but he caught me trying. He told me he liked my act. He said that even though I was not too good, he liked the fact that I wouldn't give up. That was the beginning of our long-standing association.

One time when Bob and a whole movie crew were in Puerto Rico on location making *The Private Navy of Sergeant O'Farrell*, I had a whole week off during which I rented a sailboat and had a solitary sail all around the beautiful Bahamas.

When I showed up for work after my heavenly week, Bob said: 'You're NOT going to take the money,' with that wonderful deliciously derisive mock-hostile tone of voice. I laugh every time I think about it, and all the times he's said: "I love all your faces."

He even accused me of going to a Drive-In-Face-Lift place in the Valley called THE TOOT 'N' TUCK. He said I'd had so many face lifts I entered a Phyllis Diller look-alike contest and LOST.

JOE FRANKLIN

In my mind, if I had to choose a megastar who was the most natural un-actor, who is unpretentious, untheatrical, a plain organic- from- the—bone star, it would be Bob Hope.

He's a man, even when he was on top, who would stop on the street to anybody who recognized him and kid and laugh and sign an autograph. In a night club, he would seek out the talent backstage and say nice things and encouraged other troopers.

Bob Hope and I mutually like one another. He calls me the "King of Nostalgia." And when I would try to ask him to hire some of those nostalgic stars when he had his TV show, he had to reluctantly turn me down:

"Joe," he said, "I love Benny Fields, Blossom Seeley, and guys like Arthur Tracy (The Street Singer), but my material is strictly current stuff, topical humor, so I cannot use them, as much and I would like to. My show depends upon things of the moment type material."

(photo Joe Franklin)

Bob's success has been exactly that, and has paid off for him for over 60 years. You can't argue against that. And, when Dorothy Lamour hit some hard times, he would find out she was in New York and would call me from wherever he was to ask me to put her on my show, which I did. "Give her a break, but don't tell her I had anything to do with it." And when his old sidekick Jerry Colonna was in a home in Woodland Hills, Bob was just about the only person who called him, sent him money. Jerry was once very important to Bob and he never forgot it.

Bob was not a great singer, but he sure introduced some great songs on Broadway like, "I Can't Get Started" and "It's De Lovely." He would add words like "It's deductible." He could have been a successful singer. Remember his wonderful rendition of "Thanks for the Memory" with beautiful Shirley Ross, his co-star. Name something better.

I'll never forget his calling me out from the audience in Madison Square Garden when he appeared there with George Burns. There must have been 30,000 people there:

"Ladies and gentlemen, here's a national treasure—my friend of many years—meet Joe Franklin." Who else would do that? About a year ago or so, I talked briefly to Bob from his home.

"Joe, that's all I can give you today, the old man is getting tired and cranky and I have to go and watch the fights. Dolores wants to talk with you," and she did. Dolores is the other half of Bob Hope. She adores him.

People forget that Bob Hope was number one on TV, number one on radio, number one on Broadway, number one in the movies. The first *Road* film saved Paramount. A one shot deal that nobody thought would take off—it trail blazed future movies. The improvisational ad-libbing between Crosby and Hope, with all those "inside" jokes was unheard of at the time. Bob created a lot of show business history. And, of course, traveling with all those USO shows for all those years in so many places you can't count them.

He might just be the greatest entertainer ever.

LEE HALE
BEVERLY HILLS, CALIFORNIA, JUNE 2001

Dean Martin's TV musical director for 14 years and Martin stand-in during most rehearsals. Author of the book "Backstage at the Dean Martin Show," with Richard Neely.

Bob Hope made only one appearance on the Dean Martin TV show. The year was 1966. I had put together special material for Bob and Dean to perform with dancer Juliet Prowse. Bob, like everyone who did our show, was in awe of our star because Dean never rehearsed and joined in at the last minute before taping.

Bob agreed that Dean performed better without rehearsal, although he wondered aloud why Dean's straight lines got most of the laughs during their patter. Bob was impressed and later asked me for write musical hunks for his specials. I remember I was working on a duet with him and Diana Ross one day and she was somewhat hesitant about her approach to it. It was her first time out as a single, and she wanted it to be just right! I went over it with her until she got up the nerve to rehearse it with Bob. But Bob had gone home.

That same evening I had invited Alice Faye and Florence Henderson to my house for spaghetti and in the middle of eating Bob called to say he would like me to come to his house and go over his part of the duet before Diana showed up in the morning. When I told Alice and Florence that Bob insisted I come over, she became furious, grabbed the phone and shouted, "I don't care what show you're doing, Lee is not going to bow down to your ridiculous demands to rehearse whenever you get the urge. He's going to stay here and have a nice dinner with me and Florence and you can lump it."

She slammed down the phone. A little too much of the bubbly had grandly transformed her into my champion. But I knew I'd probably never work for Bob Hope again. The next morning I arrived at Bob's house and the first words from him were,

Lee Hale with June Allyson (*Lee Hale collection*)

"Boy, that Alice has a great sense of humor. I love her. And she was right, you know." We went over the Diana Ross medley. He was pleased and Diana was totally at ease, and it all came off beautifully on the air.

Later, Bob asked me to talk to Dean's producer, Greg Garrison, about allowing the Golddiggers (dancers) to go with him on one of his USO trips to Vietnam. They did and repeated many times. Bob let me write some sexy special material for him to do with the girls. He knew how the servicemen would salivate just seeing those twelve beautiful young ladies. Yet he was a true father figure to them as well, dutifully protecting the girls from those rambunctious GIs and the sports figures Bob always took along with him.

It was great to be a small part of those tours. It was great to work with the greatest comedian and one of the greatest entertainers ever.

I worked with Bob and Dolores Hope on his last Christmas Special in 1993. Geoff Clarkson, Bob's piano player and I wrote a little song for them called "Jack Frost." Bob always claimed he knew what would work and what wouldn't and he was always right.

We all admire and love Bob Hope.

ED MCMAHON
BEVERLY HILLS, CALIFORNIA, JULY 2001

On a rainy night in August of 1943, I stood alongside my fellow aviation cadets outside the auditorium at the University of Georgia in Athens, Georgia. I was in boot camp on my way to becoming a 2nd Lieutenant in the Marine Corps...and a fighter pilot!

But standing in the rain that night, it was certainly not a "fait' accompli." The best thing we had was the news that Bob Hope and his troupe had agreed to do a second show for the cadets who waited soaking wet while the first show was in progress.

Ed McMahon with his old boss Johnny Carson
(R. Grudens collection)

We did finally get to see Bob Hope do his great thing, *Entertaining the troops*! That second show audience really dug Bob Hope and the entertainers. The fact that they were sitting there in wet uniforms didn't mean a thing.

I sat in that audience wondering if I'd ever get to be lucky enough to meet the great Bob Hope!

Many years later, I thought about this at a private luncheon I was having at Mr. Hope's house in Toluca Lake. I was there with the great man himself. He made it seem a very ordinary circumstance that he and I were having lunch. I told him about that rainy night in Georgia long ago, and as he laughed the phone rang. It was General Dwight D. Eisenhower, President and monumental hero calling to set a golf date. Bob Hope made that call seem very ordinary also.

I was then and still am a friend of Bob Hope. It doesn't get any better than this.

GEOFFREY CLARKSON
N. HOLLYWOOD, CALIFORNIA, JUNE 2001

Geoffrey Clarkson has been Bob's piano player and musical director for over 50 years.

Bob loves the laughter he generates, the cheering, the applause, the attention. He loves meeting and talking to just about everybody.

When Bob was flying within the United States, he was always accompanied by his musical director, Geoffrey Clarkson. Geoff, a longtime member of Les Brown's band from the days Les featured Doris Day as his girl singer, played the original featured piano solo on perhaps the best instrumental recording of the Big Band Era, "I've Got My Love to Keep Me Warm," and kept playing right up through Bob's USO trips. During an interview with Geoff in April, 2001, he described his association with Bob Hope:

Geoff Clarkson
A few years back
(G. Clarkson collection)

Two years after I started with Bob, I got a call from him. Right out of the blue he asked me if I would like to go to Alaska. Thinking he was planning a tour, I said, "Sure! Fine," he said, "Be at my house in half an hour." So began my first Christmas tour with Bob. Within a few hours we were on the Secretary of the Air Force's plane on the way to Anchorage.

I played with Les Brown on most of Bob's overseas Christmas tours beginning in the late forties, and had developed a good rapport with him. So, after nine years working with musical director Lee Hale on the "Dean Martin Show," which ended in 1974, Bob asked me to join him as his pianist/conductor for his live appearances, and I have happily worked with Bob ever since. I remember once when Bob and I would travel to a city where an orchestra was provided, we were flying in a Cessna Citation, a very small plane. Bob was resting in the passenger compartment and I was seated up front in the co-pilot's seat. The pilot told me that if he set a glass of water on top of the instrument panel, he could do a slow rollover and never spill a drop. We were not wearing seat belts, and centrifugal force held the water in the glass and Bob

yelled to us, "How far over did we go? never realizing we had gone completely over.

In all the years I worked with Bob, he never once lost his temper or got angry with me. He was always kind and considerate, even if I goofed up. I once forgot my music going from one place to another in a jet. Bob simply told the pilot to turn the plane around and back to Phoenix we went. He never complained or mentioned a word about it. That's the kind of a man Bob Hope is.

In 1995, Geoff played piano for Bob's "Hope for the Holidays" CD and arranged Dolores' "Somewhere in Time" album. Geoff still works with the Hope's whenever a piano player or musical director is needed.

SID CAESAR

I consider Bob Hope to a true patriot, a wonderful man, and a great comedian. Who else traveled so far and for so many years to entertain our servicemen in such dangerous places? Through every one of those wars he took chances and did his very important job, making those GI's laugh. You know, when you travel to places like Vietnam, you have to take 25 shots to protect yourself against so many possible illnesses. I don't know how many times he did that.

I played golf with Bob once, long ago in the Catskills. His partner was Sam Snead, and my partner, well never mind. You don't want to know. That was the first and last time I played with him.

When I went to Paris with Bob in 1983 for Bob's 80th birthday celebration, we encountered a fierce storm with crazy lightning, winds that could knock you off your feet, thunder-like bombs going off, and we were stuck on the tarmac for over four hours, itching to get going. Everyone was a nervous wreck, shaking. And what was Bob Hope doing? Well Bob just sat back, pulled out a book in the middle of all this mayhem and started reading like everything was okay. People on the plane were shaking. Maybe he had more experience or maybe it was just Bob being Bob Hope, the genuine icon. Here's a guy who can fall asleep anywhere, anytime, just like a kitten.

That's all I can say about Bob Hope, the great comedian and an absolutely wonderful man. I'm proud to know him.

Sid Caesar
(courtesy Movie Star News)

Frances Langford during those USO trips
(courtesy Francis Langford)

★★★★★★★★★★★★★★★★★★★★★★★★★★★★★

ACT SEVEN:
THE USO TOURS

BOB HAS BEEN THERE

....
(courtesy USO)
....

"Hello fellow tourists."

"You remember World War II, it was in all the papers"

*The Guiness Book says he traveled
ten million miles—400 times around the world.
Fifty three trips to Europe alone.*

"Bob Hope did more for the morale of the Armed Forces than any American that has ever lived." General William Westmoreland

"GOD WILLING, BOB WILL BE THERE!"

During the dark days of World War II, on remote desert airfields, aboard aircraft carriers, at subzero Alaskan outposts, and in exotic places like Owl Island, New Guinea, one exciting piece of scuttlebutt persisted:

BOB HOPE WAS COMING
OR
BOB HOPE HAS BEEN THERE

In his quest to entertain American service men and women during wars from the 1940s to the present, Bob traveled more miles than Henry Kissinger, Christopher Columbus, and Marco Polo combined, and all without regard for his own personal safety or comfort. Along the way he always had lots of company, cavorting with all the great entertainers: Bing Crosby, John Wayne, William Holden, Margaret Whiting, Clark Gable, Fred Astaire, the Andrews Sisters, Steve McQueen, Neil Armstrong, Jack Benny, Phyllis Diller, Jerry Colonna, Ann Jillian, Raquel Welch, Gina Lollobrigida, Frances Langford, Mickey Mantle, and practically every notable movie star. His association with America's military

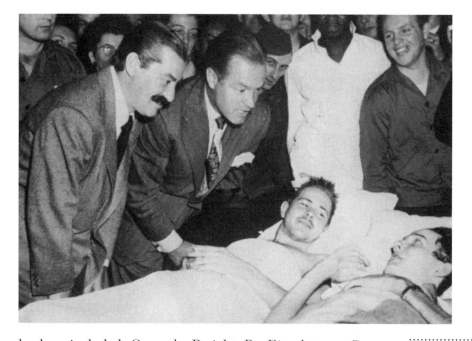

leaders included Generals Dwight D. Eisenhower, George Patton, Lucius Clay, "Hap" Arnold, Jimmy Doolittle, and Admiral William Halsey.

"It's nice to see Jimmy Doolittle again. You all know General Doolittle. He's all Air Force. He wasn't born. He was built by Boeing...."

******

Bob began his road shows for military personnel in 1941 at March Field, California, and for the next five years always broadcasted his regular radio show from military bases in the continental United States. There were over 300 performances covering bases in every state:

Bob: "There were no cameras, no lights, no group of technicians, just me, the cast, the writers, the band and two guys with a microphone. We didn't even need idiot cards. I got out there and heard those laughs, and I understood, and that's why I kept going on and on with those shows. I would find out the name of the local commanders and work them into the routine which went over very big. I

Bob and Jerry Colonna. "Don't get up for us, boys!" In 1940s at Walter Reed Hospital
(US Public Information Office)

used that formula from then on at all the shows."

Why wasn't Bob in uniform? When he decided to join up, President Roosevelt himself ordered deferments for a few vital entertainers he felt were too valuable to the Armed Forces doing what they did best—*entertain*. Bob Hope was one of those entertainers.

*****

Bob: "In 1942 we played all the glamour spots—Cold Bay, Anchorage, Cordova and Nome. Our first overseas trip was to England. We had "Mother" Frances Langford as our singer—she always knew what was best for us—Tony Romano, our guitar player, Jack Pepper, a seasoned vaudeville comedian— Colonna couldn't make it—and me."

Dorothy Lamour: "I'll never forget my first show in March Field in California with Bob. Those kids enjoyed it so much, it was like a gift from home to them. Bob would get up there and they would laugh for an hour. He just knew how to reach them to evoke laughter."

Frances Langford: "Bob had invited me to be his guest. the first time we did a show for the military, and I must say it was tremendous. So Bob said, it worked so well that maybe we should keep it going. We did. I think it lasted five years. Bob brought laughter and that's what was needed more than anything."

Top: Bob Hope brings a little laughter to the troops, here at Munda Airstrip in Munda, New Georgia, August 5, 1944 (USO photo) Bottom: Bob Hope entertaining USAF personnel in England, 1943 *(USAF-USO)*

Bob Hope: "Those troops over there, what hardships they go through. Night after night they went without sleep, always alert, always keeping their eye on their objective. Finally, Frances Langford pulled down her shade."

*****

During Bob's first USO trip overseas in 1943, when he flew with his troupe to England to entertain troops stationed there, they were still worrying about an invasion, and everything in England was secret. On the way to Sharpington Army Air Base the sky became black with returning B-17's:

"They said 18 went out and 18 came back- filling the whole countryside with the powerful vibrations of victory. This was because there had been a recent mission where 21 went out and only one limped home. Pretty grim. Soon trucks and jeeps full of fliers began rolling in, and when they saw us they began to laugh, cry and shout. To show you how brave those guys really were, they even hugged me. It made us feel great, too."

From that simple beginning the fever caught on. Next, Bob and his crew flew to Marrakech, Tunis and Algiers in North Africa. Then he carried his shows virtually everywhere, not only to the big camps.

MORE, FROM FRANCES LANGFORD

"Being the only girl in the troupe then, which was exciting in a way, I got the chance to tell stories and listen to stories from the men who were happy to see a girl from home.

"Once, in Salerno, Italy, the only bathroom was a ditch that the guys had built for me and covered around with a picket type fence and they threw in a box of Kleenex. Then I happened to look up the side of the hill on which there were a grove of olive trees. There were boys seated in every treelooking down at me. I think that was the biggest audience I ever had."

Stateside, Bob could also be heard over Command Performances USA, radio transcriptions where recordings of

Bob's and others shows were produced in the studio and then transposed onto large "V" discs and sent directly to Armed Forces overseas to be played in the field. Artists were chosen by armed forces requests sent in from military venues all over the globe. This brought to them current radio programs aimed at the men and women overseas and in remote positions.

Bob Hope and Tony Romano entertain men of the 91st Bomb Group during their visit to Bassingbourne, England on 7 July 1943 *(USAF photo)*

At the Hollywood Canteen USO Fundraiser. (Actress Joan Leslie on left) *(courtesy USO)*

THE HOLLYWOOD CANTEEN

The First Broadcast, October 13, 1942

On the tenth day after it first started the Hollywood Canteen broadcast Bob Hope's Pepsodent Radio show and featured actress Bette Davis, singer Frances Langford, funnyman Jerry Colonna, comedienne Vera Vague, and Skinnay Ennis and his Orchestra. It was the very first broadcast from the canteen:

"This is Bob "Hollywood Canteen" Hope saying everything has changed here in Hollywood. Everything is dimmed out here along the coast. Can't have any lights shining towards the sky. Even the pinball machines in the drug stores are turned upside down. But they hired a midget to stand underneath them to tell you what your score is.

"What a reception I received when I arrived at the railroad station. One very enthusiastic fan hoisted me up on his shoulders and carried me for blocks. I said, 'You are a devoted fan without equal,' and he said, 'No! I am a cabdriver without tires.'

"The canteen is great. Any enlisted man can come here and be served free food by big name Hollywood beauties. One soldier had a turkey dinner, danced with Dorothy Lamour, and spent the evening sitting on Hedy Lamarr's lap. He's been AWOL for four days now. They can't send him back to camp until he stops steaming.

"The Canteen is so popular now that I know a guy who borrowed a uniform just to get in, but they knew he was a fake because the uniform fit him...So they threw me out!

"And Dorothy Lamour almost had a disaster happen to her in the kitchen when wearing her sarong. One nearsighted soldier reached for a dish towel."

*****

In 1944, it was the battle scarred Hawaiian Islands for the "Hope Gypsies," as the players called themselves. Armed with area maps, they began their trip to the Pacific. They showed up at a group of remote islands with singer Frances Langford, and their one man band, guitar player Tony Romano, as well as dancer Patty Thomas, vaudevillian Jack Pepper and "Professor" Jerry Colonna.

*****

"Sure, our guys had won the islands we visited, but the Japanese were still in control of the suburbs. I told them, "So this is Eniwetok. What an island! It's so small, when the tide comes in, you guys should get submarine pay...You're not defending this place, are you? Let them take it, it'll serve them right!" It felt good to bring girls and music and laughs to places where the only thing breaking the monotony before was finding a new fungus growing on you."

*****

In 1945, the valiant troupe headed back to England, France and Germany.

During the Korean conflict Bob Hope's first USO show that would be shown on television was staged in Thule, Greenland in 1954. It featured beautiful Anita Ekberg, then Miss UCLA, vocalist Margaret Whiting, comedian Jerry Colonna, actor Bill Holden, Hollywood columnist Hedda Hopper, actor Peter Leeds, and Les Brown and his Band of Renown.

It became Bob's first of many televised Christmas specials. Six thousand troops, under the command of Bob's friend, General Rosie O'Donnell, who provided transportation for the troupe of entertainers, were treated to a full scale show, to be followed by a New Year's Eve show from Goose Bay, Labrador, also before a vast uniformed crowd. Here, Bob had found a comedian's radio and television niché that would carry his career forward many years into the future to legendary, world-wide fame.

"I slept in the barracks last night. You know what barracks are—that's two thousand cots separated by individual crap games"

Bob and his troupe performed even from the back of trucks in those days. Anywhere would due. In North Africa, they were invited by General George Patton to Palermo, Sicily, three days after the city of Messina fell to the Allies. They landed and were driven to Palermo to perform for the men who had been injured in the assault. They well realized the value of the USO shows after that.

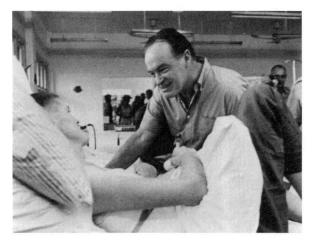

"It allowed our fighting men to vent their feelings and fears through jokes and diversions our little group put on for them.

"We did one show in the middle of a volcano in Milne Bay in the South Pacific. We did the whole pineapple circuit, from Honolulu to Eniwetok. Hell, I remember a show in 1945 when the Japs offered to surrender. We were in Nuremberg, Germany, at the Olympic Stadium, when the announcement came. The whole stadium full of guys seemed to rise 20 feet in the air. Nothing could ever compare to a moment like that. It's pretty hard to upstage."

*****

There were many close calls for Bob Hope and his troupe of players. In North Africa, just outside of Bizerte, a couple of tracer bullets came pretty close over their heads. An MP kept yelling at them and had them take cover in a sewer. When they got back to their hotel afterwards, it was partially bombed out.

"The next shower I had was when I ran into a wet sheep dog."

In Bizerte they witnessed the downing of a German plane that appeared to be coming down on top of them, but fortunately crashed in a nearby field.

"It was scary the first time seeing our boys shot up—their feet or arms just ragged chunks of meat. Those guys really gave for their country. Sometimes you thought the noise alone would kill you when a bomb landed nearby. When 100 planes are in the air throwing a lot of stuff, it's a frightening experience, and I've sat through many Phyllis Diller monologues."

In 1948, Irving Berlin went to Germany during the airlift with Bob and his troupe to uplift the morale of the American airmen stationed there. Jinx Falkenburg and Tex McCrary, who had a Mr. & Mrs. breakfast radio show on NBC in New York, comedienne Irene Ryan, who later played Granny on the *Beverly Hillbillies* TV show, three writers including Larry Gelbart, and General Jimmy Doolittle, went along.

"We had a nice trip from America. Irving Berlin came with us. He didn't help our morale any. All the way across he kept singing, "How Deep Is the Ocean." Irving doesn't have the best voice, either. He sounds like a rusty hinge in search of a can of 3-in-1 oil.

"And the people over here really know me. Whenever I walk down the streets of Berlin, everybody follows me yelling and cheering. Any of you fellows know what *Schweinehund* means?"

"Here we are in West Berlin—that's a PX surrounded by Russians. And what a contrast going from West Berlin to East Berlin. It's like giving up Rhonda Fleming for Ma Kettle."

An interesting aside to this story is when Bob was invited to visit a local radio station manned by Staff Sergeant Robert Kelso of Armed Forces Radio upon an invitation earlier in the day when Kelso intercepted Bob after the Berlin show. Kelso had implored him, since many of the guys who couldn't see the show would like to hear Bob speak directly to them over local radio.

After a midnight party on the way back to their hotel, Bob suddenly remembered the invitation and had the driver of his car drive over to the radio station (the last few blocks by foot, as it was snowing and the car also ran out of gas.) When Bob and Dolores showed up Sergeant Kelso couldn't believe it. He was stunned.

"Oh my God!" he turned to the mike and said, "Hey, guys! Have I got news for you. It's the one and only Bob Hope. He's here! I'm turning the mike over to him."

Kelso disappeared after pouring some coffee for Dolores, and Bob did his monologue for his faithful servicemen. After a while, Bob wondered where Kelso went. It turned out that he had run over to wake up other disc jockeys at nearby Armed Forces Radio returning after a half-hour or so.

"Who otherwise would have believed me if I told them Bob Hope dropped in on me at two-thirty in the morning the day after Christmas?"

Bob Hope did lots of things like that.

*****

On a trip to Russia, Bob had lots of ammunition in the jokes. "The Ukraine is not a regular Intourist hotel but is usually reserved for the top agriculturists and leaders of trade delegations in the U.S.S.R. And as we walked in, the lobby was swinging with hundreds of pajama-clad Uzbeks and Mongolians, intent on a bacchanalian weekend at the ball bearing works."

Back in the States a reporter asked if they had television in russia, and without thinking Bob replied, "Yes. but it watches you."

Bob arrived in Red Square, the heart of Moscow. "At the South end of the square is St. Basil's Cathedral with its nine onion-shaped domes, Russia's answer to Disneyland. And the GUM department store makes Macy's look like the general store in Upper Sandusky. I tried to buy one of those fur hats like I'd seen the men wearing on the street. Then I found out those aren't hats. That's the way they cut their hair."

*****

In Korea, Bob met with South Korean President Syngman Rhee in Seoul. It was the first time Bob flew in a jet plane. There were 10,000 guys there to meet him and Marilyn Maxwell, and they worked the entire area right up to the 38th parallel. The guys really reacted to Marilyn. Bob said they wanted him to leave and her to stay.

"Everywhere we went we had 25 MPs guarding the girls and a midget with a slingshot for us guys. But really, we did have security for every member of the crew. We always moved

in convoy. There were always Jeeps in front and Jeeps in back of us."

Aboard the Aircraft Carrier Shangri-La, anchored off Naples, Italy 1963:

"It's a thrill to be here on the U.S.S. Crapgame. The Navy calls it Shangri-La, but that's just for the winners. I've never seen such action. I sat down at a mess table and the sugar cubes had numbers on them. And I've never heard of a chaplain wearing a green eye-shade before."

In 1964, after months of trying to arrange it, Bob finally received word from the Pentagon that he would be allowed to make his first Christmas trip to the Vietnam war zone, where he faced the same dangers as he did during World War II. He continued his travels right through the crisis in Lebanon and Operation Desert Storm in the Persian Gulf.

"I visited a mosque when I was here six years ago. On this trip I plan to visit them again. It's not that I'm overly religious, I just wanna get my shoes back."

BOB HOPE SHOW 1966 CU CHI, VIETNAM
KEVIN O'HARE 25TH DIV. SPECIAL SERVICES

Kevin's job was to act as warmup MC.
"I arrived in Cu Chi in November 1966 attached to the 25th Division Commanders Office under General Frederick C. Weyland and was offered a job to boost morale, thus I was

assigned to Special Services. My first assignment w[...] Bob Hope's Christmas Show. My previous backgroun[...] vision as assistant producer for both Soupy Sales [...] "Wonderama Show" with Sonny Fox, helped me m[...] assignment.

"Part of the job was to control seating, the firs[...] being held for wounded soldiers and other rows fo[...] VIP's.

"Behind the scenes, Phyllis Diller is having problems with her hair because of unusual high humidity; Bob Hope is taking an after rehearsal nap, after downing some chips. He is kind of nervous today, as the show was under fire from the enemy; Joey Heatherton was grateful to see me, an old school friend of her brother; Diller asked to be flown back to base in a larger helicopter (2 blades instead of the smaller huey's) which we were able to grant.

"During the show I noticed the mood of the soldiers was somber, as most had thoughts of home. It was to be difficult to face action especially after Bob Hope sang 'Thanks for the Memory.' All the entertainers became very emotional by the end of the show. They (Hope's crew) hated to leave. So did the soldiers. After the show, Bob Hope and the cast visited the wounded in area hospitals. It was an uplifting experience for those men, too.

"On the way back, Bob Hope realized the VC attempted to break through the perimeter before the show had started. American soldiers killed two VC and a captured a third who had actually sneaked through. My job was to get the audience in a good frame of mind and forget the war for the next one and a half hours.

"It was a great time in my life emceeing some of these shows for the Bob Hope troupe and seeing my fellow soldiers receive some enjoyment. Many of those guys never came back. Today, I fight for veterans rights as a member of several vet organizations. I will never forget those guys and Bob Hope, the great entertainer, who also risked his life to give those guys the break they needed. Those men appreciated it. They told me they were grateful.

"Bob...you're the best. Thanks for OUR memories."

*****

Dolores Hope

Anita Bryant

Joey Heatherton

Kevin O'Hare
with Vic
Damone,
Vietnam, 1966

At the Brinks Hotel in Vietnam, there was an attack just minutes before Bob and his troupe arrived on a Christmas Eve. Two Americans were killed and fifty were wounded. Some years later a document was found that proved the bomb was meant for Bob Hope and his troupe. Luckily they arrived late.

"We did a party for the victims of the blast. I grabbed Colonna and Les Brown and headed out the door when Garrick Utley of NBC News asked me to do the show at the naval hospital where the victims of the blast were recuperating. It was at the direct request of General Westmoreland. Some of the people were riddled with glass when they were caught in the shower when the bomb blew. One kid with blood streaming down his face looked up at me when someone called out 'Bob Hope,' and he shouted 'Merry Christmas!'" I'll never forget that as long as I live, because he meant it.

"I fell asleep that night during midnight mass Cardinal Spellman was saying. When I met him at the airport a couple of days later, I apologized, and he said, 'That's all right, don't worry about it. I once caught your act at Loew's State.'"

*****

Bob: Here she is....Miss Raquel Welch

(Music for Raquel) (applause)

Bob: At ease, at ease...Stop drooling...you're increasing the humidity, you fools.

Raquel: Bob, am I standing in the right place.

Bob: Honey, don't worry...if you're not...we'll move the base.

Raquel: Well, thank you. I'm most happy to be here and see all these boys.

Bob: They were boys before you came out. Now they're old men.

Raquel: We should talk about you, you're the real hero here.

Bob: Who told you that?

Raquel: You did!

*****

In 1965 Bob was off to Thailand, and Vietnam again, as he would be for the next five years with many stars joining up with him: Joey Heatherton, Mickey Mantle, Johnny Bench, Eddie Fisher, and Connie Stevens, to name a few.

The late 1960s found Bob and his troupe traveling to the South Pacific and aboard hospital ship *Sanctuary* in the China Sea; on the USS New Jersey in Vietnam, in Incirli, Turkey, and in the 1970s in Souda Bay, Crete; Hanau, Germany; Osan AFB, Korea; aboard the USS John Kennedy in Crete and the USS Midway in Singapore; Namphong, Thailand, Diego Garcia in the Indian Ocean and aboard the USS Okinawa in the Persian Gulf in 1988.

*****

"Here we are in beautiful Thailand. In October you get the monsoons. In December you get me. Things are so tough here that one cobra had to lay off three flute players."

APPRECIATIVE SERVICEMEN WHO WERE THERE SPEAK UP

Lt. John D. Saint, Jr.
Somewhere in South Africa 1943

"It was not officially announced that I know of, but the word spread like wildfire, 'Bob Hope is in town.' There were maybe fifteen thousand guys there. All of a sudden Hope came in riding in a command car followed by two more. There he was, famous nose sunburned. He brought out Jack Pepper and Tony Romano, and they were great. And then Frances Langford appeared. She sang from the bottom of her heart, 'You Made me Love You' and 'Embraceable You.' Every one of those thousands of men went home to their wives and sweethearts for a moment. There was not a sound and there was not a movement. She will never know what it did to us. It was almost more than a man could stand."

*****

Peter Beck, PFC, Combat engineers
Anyang-Ni, near Seoul, Korea 1951.

Peter landed at Inchon, fought battles at Sanju, Yonju, Wonju, and ChipYon Nee. His unit installed many pontoon and baily bridges across rivers to support the other troops. He now resides in Nissequogue, New York.

Peter Beck with South Korean soldier *(P. Beck collection)*

"We first heard that Bob Hope's show was coming through a notice in Stars & Stripes. Like many of us, we had to hitch-hike or find some way of getting to the large amphitheater 20 to 30 miles or so away to see Bob with his show. You had to bring a blanket or something to sit on or you sat on dirt. We were all very excited. Besides our guys, there were Scots, British troops, Australian and even Turks, that came to see the show.

"I brought my camera along but was too far away from the stage area to get a good photo. It was a great show and it made us feel better. There was no entertainment at all where we were stationed, so a live show Bob Hope style was what we needed. That's what we got!

"I became a big Bob Hope fan after that, and when I got home, I

hardly missed a Bob Hope movie or television special. I felt he was a friend. I eventually got my photo of him when he appeared at Westbury Music Fair on Long Island, some years later."

Ted Kaplan,
Private First Class, Ground photographer

Graduate of the Army Air Force Technical Training School at Lowry Field, Denver, Colorado, was assigned to the 32nd Photo Reconnaissance Squadron, Gainesville Air Force Base, Gainesville, Florida.

Shutterbug Kaplan, Lowry Field, Denver, Colorado, 1943

"When word came that Bob Hope was arriving with his compliment of performers for a USO show, and I was awarded that plum assignment, I couldn't believe my luck.

"An hour before Hope and his crew arrived, excited servicemen and women, anticipating the show of a lifetime, took their seats in front of a temporary stage set up outside an airplane hanger and waited for Bob's arrival: Who would he bring? And would anyone from the audience be invited onstage as a foil for his comedy?

"Well, Bob did not disappoint. To ever-growing thunderous applause, whistles, and cheers, Hope introduced in turn Frances Langford, actress Jane Wyman (Ronald Reagan's first wife), Tony Romano, and Jerry Colonna. What a show they gave us! Best of all, at the top of his form, was Bob himself. He made everyone feel that he was speaking to, and clowning with, that person, teasing the audience in that warm and relaxed way that only Bob could accomplish.

"I had gotten some okay shots of each performer, and then I had an idea. In our outfit was a Native American, known to one and all as Chief. The Chief was the real thing—the leader of a genuine American Indian tribe. I knew the Chief wanted

to present Bob with an authentic, regal Indian headdress of feathers. Only people considered to be leaders in their own right, or persons counted as friends of the tribe would ever be awarded such an honor.

"Hope was in an ebullient mood, and the show had gone well, the audience showering him with adoration. I guided the Chief onto the stage and positioned myself for the shot. Hope, of course, was happy to be photographed as he was presented the headdress. The band played "Hail to the Chief" as directed by Bob. The audience stood and cheered, and I got my shot of them smiling as they faced one another. A shot that I will always remember and be proud of.

"I'll never forget that show, or Bob Hope's graceful way of making the occasion work so well! Thanks for the memory, Bob."

Major Bruce Kates
USAF Public Information Officer for the 1333rd

Troop Carrier Wing assigned to Fassberg AFB, Germany, during the Berlin Airlift. Bruce was responsible for arranging facilities for the Bob Hope Christmas Tour, December 23-24, 1948 Major Kates lives in Austin, Texas.

In my assignment, I had to arrange for Bob Hope and his troupe, that included Bob and Dolores Hope, Irving Berlin, Jinx Falkenberg and her husband Tex McCrary, Irene Ryan, and six Rockettes dancers, Tony Romano, among others, to use the Base Theater for the show and sleeping quarters for the cast.

When the show began, Bob entered from the rear of the theater and was being chased by Military Police as he tossed

cigarettes to the audience (big black market items, then). He bolted up onto the stage and went backstage. The Rockettes did their routine, and Tony Romano and others then entertained the audience until Bob reappeared and performed a great show.

That evening, Bob and Dolores remained behind while the rest of the cast, escorted by the Officers of the Wing drove out to a place called Flynn's Inn. This was formerly a German Hunting Lodge about 15 miles away. It had 18 bedrooms, a dance floor and kitchen. Bob went up into the Fassberg Tower and began contacting pilots on the Airlift. He told jokes and quipped with them about delivering coal and supplies to Berlin. Very funny and a great morale boost for the pilots and crews who could not attend the show at the base. He remained there until midnight while the rest of us had a great meal that included champagne at Flynn's Inn.

About midnight, Bob and his wife began to drive out to the Inn with the Wing Executive Officer in his staff car. But they ran out of gas about halfway there and on a very cold night, and had to get out and hitchhike a ride back to the Inn. A 6x6 military truck finally picked them up and brought them to the Inn. When they came through the door, I turned from the table and told Bob he needed food, because I noticed he was almost blue with the severe cold. Bob's response was, 'To hell with the food, where is the booze?'

I will never forget the wonderful show they performed for us and how much of a morale lift it was for the officers and Airmen, including a company of the British Air Force whose base we were on.

Bob Hope always gave his best to the military forces and it will never be forgotten.

*****

"THANKS FOR THE MEMORY"
(special edition)

*Read in Congress on Bob's 75th Birthday on
May 28, 1978 by minority Whip Robert Michel
the first time a song was ever sung in Congress*

> Thanks for the memory
> Of places you have gone
> To cheer our soldiers on
> The President sent Kissinger
> But you sent Jill St.John
> We thank you so much
>
> Thanks for the memories
> We honor you today
> And this is what we say,
> Thank God you left Old England
> and came to the U.S.A.
> We thank you sooooo much
>
> (THEN added)
> Seventy plus five is now your age, Bob,
> We're glad to see you still upon the stage, Bob,
> We hope you make a decent living, Bob,
> For the more you make-
> The more we take!

At which point House Speaker "Tip" O'Neil declared, "He is a fine American, he is a great American, he is an all-American. Happy birthday, Bob Hope."

They say that Dolores at his side faced him applauding, daughters Linda and Nora were crying. Kelly, Bob's brother Fred, and all the grandchildren beamed.

It's a fact that Bob Hope has been honored more than any other human being.

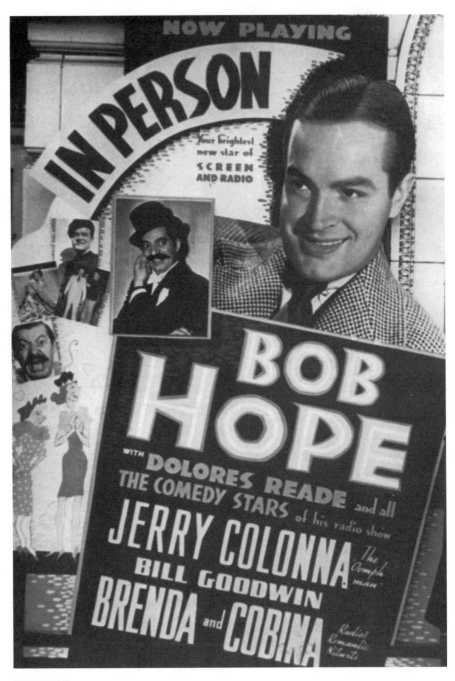

(NBC photo)

★★★★★★★★★★★★★★★★★★★★★★★★★★★★★★★★★

ACT EIGHT:
ELEVEN PRESIDENTS

E V E R Y   O N E   L A U G H I N G

With President John F. Kennedy, Air Force Secretary Stuart Symington *(White House photo)*

"I've known and entertained eleven Presidents and slept at my favorite Bed & Breakfast in Washington."

"To all the Presidents who have extended me friendship and tolerance, or who have shared a day on the golf course, a night in the White House, or an afternoon in the Rose Garden....and a lifetime of laughter. Thanks to all of them who have remained my friends even after what I said about them. They all laughed and enjoyed every bit of it. Maybe they didn't understand the jokes."

FRANKLIN DELANO ROOSEVELT

It was Franklin D. Roosevelt who first interested Bob Hope in poking fun at presidents. Bob was careful to make an insult humorous, just "denting" the presidential ego, not to damage it. And, it was President Roosevelt who first asked Bob to entertain the troops overseas during World War II.

"He asked me because he said I was popular, talented, and expendable."

President Franklin D. Roosevelt *(White House photo)*

HARRY TRUMAN

Bob, about the Truman/Dewey race for the White House:
"This campaign promises to be a hot battle. Truman has announced that he's not going to leave the White House, and Dewey says he's moving in. That'll be a nice situation...I can just see the towels in the White House bathroom....marked 'his' and 'his.'"

"Never trust a haberdasher...it frightens a lot of people. Never trust a politician who knows how to measure your inseam."

Truman: "The White House is the finest prison in the world....I guess they make license plates in the Lincoln Bedroom."

After Truman left office, he and Bess visited Bob after a show in Kansas City and invited him to Independence. Bob made the short trip to their home. As he

left, the former President shook Bob's hand and said, "Drop in anytime, will ya?" "I got the feeling that he was lonesome. He missed the action in Washington."

"Harry Truman didn't care about image. That's because he had a weapon that could bring the world to its knees—his daughter Margaret's singing voice."

Harry Truman
(White House photo)

DWIGHT D. EISENHOWER

Dwight D. Eisenhower *(photo Movie Star News)*

"Once, after Bob and his company had been subject to a bombing raid in the town of Bizerte (Tunisia), while enter-

taining our troops, he came back to Algiers where I promised him a night of peace and rest. Imagine my embarrassment when, on that very night, we had a raid on Algiers and Bob had to resign himself to a couple of hours in a dark wine cellar."

BOB: "Wasn't that a wonderful meeting at the White House between Eisenhower and Kennedy? Eisenhower said, 'Congratulations on your victory,' and Kennedy said, 'I had to win. It's so tough these days to find a place that'll take children.'"

JOHN KENNEDY

John Kennedy
(White House photo)

"President Kennedy spent the night at Bing Crosby's house. He wanted to see how the rich live. And Bing, he wants to put down the President's visit as a tax deduction."

Kennedy: "The first time I saw you, Bob, was on Wendy Island (In the South Pacific) during World War II when you gave a performance for those of us in the Navy there. Thank you for the laughs, Bob.

"And two generations of Americans raise their glasses and say to you, 'Thanks for the Memory.'"

Hope: "In September 1962, President Kennedy presented me with the Congressional Gold Medal in the White House Rose Garden:

"'Mr. President,' I said, 'I feel very humble but I think I have the strength of character to fight it. There is one sobering thought—I received this medal for going out of the country. I think they're trying to tell me something.'"

During his life, Bob had many trips to Washington, D.C. From time to time he would get a call from Kennedy's press agent Pierre Salinger, saying, "The boss would like to see you." They were casual visits for Bob where he exchanged jokes with the President. On one of the visits Kennedy told Bob one of his favorite jokes:

"An Irishman died. His widow walked around the coffin and said, 'He looks so good. And his toupee is on so straight. How did they do that?' And someone answered, 'With a nail.'"

And from Bob's television monologue in 1963:

"President Kennedy is just winding up a nonpolitical tour of the eleven states he lost in the last election. He wanted to see how they're getting along without federal aid."

In November 1963 *Camelot* ended with death of President John Kennedy:

"I never forget that dynamic man who had the quickest wit of all the presidents. Laughter was a major part of the Kennedy persona and that is the image that prevails. And I'll always remember the day in the White House Rose Garden when I, Dolores, Tony, Kelly, Nora, and Linda were the guests of President Kennedy. We were all thrilled."

LYNDON JOHNSON

"President Johnson says he wants to get started on his 'Great Society'. I don't know exactly how it's gonna work, but I think he wants Texas to adopt the rest of us."

"One of the things that LBJ likes to do is to drive at unholy speeds across the state of Texas. Well, he was doing about 95 when this cop pulls him over and, without looking, starts to write him a ticket. As LBJ cranked down the window, the stricken officer realized his mistake and said, 'Oh, my God!' and the President snapped, 'You'd better believe it.'"

President Johnson spoke about Bob Hope at

Lyndon Johnson *(White House photo)*

a Washington hotel when Bob was to receive the USO Silver Medal:

"Mr. Chairman...Mr. Bob Hope...ladies and gentlemen...

I have come here today to honor a man with two very unusual traits.

He is an actor, who is not, as far as I know, running for public office.

It may come as a surprise to some people with short memories that Bob Hope is more than a comedian. The book about his travels to entertain the troops during World War II was called 'I Never Left Home.'

Since then he has spent so much time with our troops overseas that there are those who now say he ought to write a sequel, 'I Never Came Back.'

"And we all know that wherever American men fight for freedom, there will always be Hope. And Bob, two generations of Americans raise their glasses and say to you, 'Thanks for the Memories,' ...from a grateful nation.'"

RICHARD NIXON

Richard Nixon
(NBC photo)

Bob Hope always remained loyal to his old friend, President Richard Nixon.

"The man had one of the finest minds of any President I've known. Also, he was a friend and I stand by my friends, no matter. And our noses were very much alike."

Bob was a staunch friend of Richard Nixon throughout all the troubled years of his administration. Present at Nixon's first appearance after his resignation held at the Palm Springs home of Walter Annenberg, a former Ambassador to London, Nixon spoke to the guests about the value of friendship. It was very emotional.

"He didn't talk about the past. He said that friends were very important when you are at the top, but more so at a time like his fall from grace.....he had all of us in tears."

Everyone was confounded concerning Bob's support for Nixon. But, Bob revealed a new side of himself to others. Talk about Bob being a political opportunist, stopped short. Through President Richard Nixon, Bob cultivated a friendship with his Vice President, President Gerald Ford, that still exists.

GERALD FORD

"I love playing golf with Jerry Ford. If you beat him, he pardons you."

"Over the years my friendship with Bob Hope has brought me a lot of needed laughs. He is a really nice guy and easy to get along with."

Ironically, in 1936 when Bob was appearing in "Red, Hot and Blue," a Broadway musical, the show arrived first for its try-out in New Haven, Connecticut. One of the those who congratulated Bob backstage was a young Yale law student named Jerry Ford.

"It's not hard to find Jerry Ford on a golf course" according to Bob, "You just follow the wounded. He has made golf a contact sport—he's the hit man for the PGA."

Gerald and
Betty Ford
(NBC photo)

JIMMY CARTER

"When I was in office for 489 days...I had three weeks to go, having stayed overnight in the White House as many times as Bob Hope has. I believe I was the only person in the Armed Forces who'd never met him while overseas. Every Christmas Eve we would wait in our submarine, but Bob Hope never showed up.

"As the President of the United States, there is no way for me to add additional plaques already received from my predecessor.

"So, I would just like to say 'thank you' to my friend Bob Hope."

Jimmy Carter
(NBC photo)

"What a kick it is to shake hands with the President and the First Lady...thank you, President and Mrs. Carter, for loaning us your house...God knows, we paid for it."

Ronald Reagan
(USO photo)

RONALD REAGAN

"I was a little surprised when I was asked to be here tonight to honor Bob Hope. Well, 'surprised' isn't exactly the word—I was annoyed. Now, in accepting this invitation, I don't want the taxpayers to think that I'd make a special trip down here just to be on this program.

"Now, that would be frivolous. I just happened to be in town anyway, for something really important—a guest shot on 'Hollywood Squares.'"

"Dolores and I have known Ronald and Nancy for a long time: when he was an actor; President of the Screen Actors Guild; Governor of California, and President of the United States. It's not his fault he could never hold a job."

George Bush

Bob knew George Bush's father, Prescott, and even played golf with him. He became very close to George and played a lot of golf with him, too. When he introduced Bush at a Victory dinner in 1988 in Los Angeles, he tested Bush with some one liners.

"At age two, George Bush said his first words: 'How am I doing in the polls?' When Governor Dukakis was a boy, he lived in a poor neighborhood. When George was a boy, his father showed him a picture of one."

"Bush has been sworn in, and the country will do just fine. But I still can't picture Reagan in an unemployment line. Bush is so sports minded that after the inauguration yesterday, when he swore on the Bible, he went inside and swore again on the 'Sporting News.'"

Bill Clinton

"Bill Clinton became a show business performer when he did a walk-on during my show at the University of Arkansas. He was Governor. He was a new face on the scene and was able to beat out Bush and Quayle.

"All the candidates are coming to California. Clinton is trying to convince Californians that he's one of them

Yesterday, he held a press conference while hangin' ten in the surf off Malibu.

"President Clinton is looking forward to entertaining leaders from other countries. I just hope Boris Yeltsin likes okra and catfish."

President Clinton: "Bob, stop by the next time you are in Washington. I need some advice with my back swing. More important, if, like me, you have to spend this much time in the Capitol, I need your gift of laughter."

Hillary: Bob is welcome to the White House anytime.

Bill Clinton: He's welcome, all right, but we have started counting the towels.

Hillary: Bob has needled Bill about his saxophone playing, eating at McDonald's, his jogging, his golf. I never realized Bob Hope and I had so much in common.

★★★★★★★★★★★★★★★★★★★★★★★★★★★★★★★

ACT NINE:
AT HOME

ONCE IN AWHILE

The Hopes— Bob, Dolores, Linda, Tony, Nora, Kelly *(photo Gene Lester)*

"I wanted to make sure I had a house that wasn't too big to hook onto the Super Chief if I needed to move East."

It was in 1938, following Bob's success in his first feature movie, *The Big Broadcast of 1938*, when Bob and Dolores Hope purchased a fifteen room, two story English style house with three adjacent cottages on six and three quarter acres in Toluca Lake, in the San Fernando Valley, overlooking a personal golf course with views of downtown Burbank, beyond the over ten foot hedges that surround the property. They also own a large home in Palm Springs. During Bob's lengthy travels, Dolores remodeled the entire house, both in and out. Today, a twenty foot brick wall surrounds the abode with wooden electronically operated gates to secure their privacy. The family dogs(including two white German Shepherds) act as guard dogs. I would hate to think how many people would be ringing the front door bell if it were easily available to intrusive index finger's The great oak door, opening to a spacious hall, would experience something like the daily action at the White House, with possibly thousands visiting daily. The Hope's would have to hire a tour guide.

Bob's library is stacked with books from floor to ceiling. An original portrait, crafted by renowned artist Norman Rockwell, depicts Bob as a baggy-pants comedian swinging a five iron on Bob's hallowed ground, a golf course. The mansion is named the "Hope House" by servants, among which at any given time are a cook, a maid, and a gardener—who sometimes doubles as a general repair man. A separate building houses Bob and Dolores' respective secretaries quarters, who open mail, catalogue and send mail. It also accommodates Bob's vault full of files and jokes.

*****

"I must have told a million jokes on radio—I don't remember them all, but you can check with Milton Berle, he still has them."

*****

A walk-in vault contains Bob's discs, tapes and all previously written material on paper, filed and cross-referenced in a vast subject matter index.

"I almost never use that safe, anymore. It's more a reference, or rather a trip down memory lane, where I can check

The Hope's
North
Hollywood
Home, 1953
(Mitoch and
Sons photo)

out my old-time style of how I operated back right after the Earth cooled. When I am home, I am usually on the phone, sometimes taking over a hundred calls a day. I can get a lot done that way. I always try to answer my own calls, but I leave the correspondence to the girls."

Endless awards and trophies grace Bob's office. An honorary Oscar; and the Medal of Honor, presented to him by President Kennedy, take center stage surrounded by hundreds of gifts, honors, and academic degrees, including the coveted 1978 degree from Gonzaga University, where his friend Bing Crosby attended college... way back when.

"The joke around here is 'I've been married for over seventy-five years and I've been home two months,' 'and Dolores' joke is, 'If you see Bob—say hello!'

Then Dolores would say, "I've invited all our friends to the house for Christmas, and they are all going to be dressed in camouflage—so Bob will feel at home."

Actually, Dolores accompanied Bob on a number of the USO tours; 1948 to Europe; 1949 Alaska; 1966, in the heat of the Vietnam crisis, and four other tours including one to Saudi Arabia during Desert Storm in 1991.

"Bob is a very hard worker," says Dolores, "Don't ever be fooled by his relaxed, easy-going manner. Underneath that smooth, unruffled exterior is one of the hardest working guys you have ever met. It's been that way ever since I've known him and it will be that way until the day he dies. We both feel half our ages, because we're happy, fulfilled, contented people who enjoy the day-to-day challenge of being alive."

Some people say that Bob will fall asleep while someone else is talking, but never when he is talking.

Their rare moments together, for maybe an hour or so, consists of catching up on small talk.

"We have had little time for a truly private life," says Dolores.

"Dolores is my best friend. She is very strict with me. I check out everything with her before I make a decision. If she doesn't like it...no matter what it is about..I think twice before I say yes or no."

Today, Bob is healthy but a bit frail. He attended Rosemary Clooney's marriage to Dante DiPaolo in November of 1997. Ward Grant says Bob wants to live to be 100 years like his grandfather, James Hope. He keeps moving, and when he sings, you can see the twinkle in his eye." Bob still follows what he learned as a song and dance man. Ward says Bob has his bad days, but he can still sing a song like "It's De-Lovely," a song Rosemary Clooney says is one of the most difficult pieces of music to sing correctly.

At this writing Dolores Reade Hope is 93. When she was 88 she shared the stage with her friend Rosemary Clooney at Rainbow and Stars (formerly the Rainbow Room), a night club high up on the 65th floor of Rockefeller Center. That year Dolores received a star on the Hollywood Walk of Fame. Red Buttons talked and sang their alma mater's song from Evander Childs High School in the Bronx, which they both attended.

Dolores Hope has been also honored with six honorary doctorates, has been Honorary Mayor of Palm Springs five different times. She is an outstanding philanthropist and supports many charities. She has been doing these kinds of things while Bob has been traveling the globe. Bob supports her in every venture. She is well loved, too. I've also heard her golf score is two points lower than her husband's. Not bad for a comedian's wife. Besides all of that, she helps with their four grandchildren.

Family Ties

"A house is not a house without a child in it."

Linda Hope: "Do your funny dance, Daddy."

Bob says that Dolores feels more deeply about family than he does.

"When we found out that Dolores couldn't have children, Dolores pressed me about adoption. I wasn't too keen about the idea. I was content with a wife, golf, and show business. After five years of being nudged, I visited The Cradle, a great adoption agency in Evanston, Illinois. They checked us over with a microscope, and they told Dolores that they thought I wasn't serious about wanting a child. Dolores reassured them saying 'He's just trying to appear disinterested. He's afraid he'll seem soft.'

"My celebrity status meant nothing to them," said Bob.

The Hopes first adopted Linda, and in a year they added Tony. Dolores wanted even more kids, and the *Cradle* found both Nora and Kelly for them. Dolores was ecstatic. Bob wondered if he belonged to the kids or if the kids belonged to him.

"Once, I laughed my head off when Kelly asked our youngest, Nora, 'Is everybody in our family catholic?' 'Yes,' Nora said, 'everybody but Daddy. He's a comedian.' She could

Bob and Dolores with grandson Zachary *(courtesy Look Magazine)*

have been one of my writers. I was their Daddy, but sometimes I had trouble convincing them that I'm a comedian."

When the kids would see Bob step out the door each morning when he was spending time at home, they would say something like, 'Do your funny dance, Daddy.' So Bob established a routine that consisted of a couple of dance shuffles. Halfway to his car, he would do it again. And sometimes Bob was surprised when the children would greet him with, after Bob says ..."Good Morning", children! they replied, "Good morning, Bob Hope."

"So I cautioned them to not say such things when we were in public, so Linda said, 'We know, Daddy. We're supposed to let you get all the laughs.'"

Sometimes the kids traveled with Bob and Dolores on the USO tours. One of the great stories centered around Nora. Some ten thousand troops had gathered in the hot sun to see the show. Medics said they expected lots of cases of heat prostration, so hospital towels were soaked in ice water. Nora became the runner for the towels to keep members of the band cool. Not one member had a problem, thanks to Nora.

That was a number of years ago, of course, and the kids are no longer kids. These days Linda runs Hope Enterprises and Tony runs his own law practice. Nora and Kelly are living their lives more privately, away from tabloids and telephones. Grandchildren Zach Hope, Andrew Lande, Miranda Hope, and Robert Hope, are her best critics and best fans.

Dolores Hope was honored with "The Winds Beneath My Wings" Award from the Betty (sister of Rosemary) Clooney Foundation.

★★★★★★★★★★★★★★★★★★★★★★★★★★★★

ACT TEN:
OSCARS AND EMMY'S
AND OTHER HONORS

The Academy Awards "At our house is known as Passover." *(courtesy Academy of Motion Pictures Art and Sciences.)*

*"The Academy Awards nominations are out...and so am I.
I don't mind not being nominated, but even the tourist bus
doesn't stop at my house anymore."*

Despite the fact that Bob Hope is probably the most celebrated entertainer of all time, a household name known worldwide for over 75 years, he has never received an Emmy, an Oscar, or any other award for being "Best Comedian," although he has received a number of honorary Oscars and Emmys.

So, why do we love and enjoy Bob Hope so much? Well, his jokes always hit home because he carefully engineers it that way. His self denigration wins him sympathy, converted to laughs from an audience. He sets it up: First he brags, then he tears himself down, stares, and waits. It always works. He is the master of the one liners, even greater than all the other one-liner comedians. That's why he is acknowledged to be the best by all his peers.

Further, Bob Hope's success is due partly to his unique delivery. Try having someone else deliver jokes exactly as he does. It will not work. It cannot work. They are formulated and fitted by him. Jack Benny similarly won laughs exercising his famous stare after delivering a comedy line. Then he simply waited for the audience to react. Part of Bob's success is an ability to study and know his audience, angling his jokes to befit the audience's mood, background, or current connecting event. No one does impressions of Bob Hope.

"I edited all the jokes my guys have written for me over the years. I drove those guys hard. You have to know what the audience will accept and appreciate. If I didn't know what was good material and what was bad to present, I would have been in lots of trouble. I found an acceptable formula and put it to work, probably never altering it very much. I have to admit that without writers I could not have done it alone. Writers write but cannot deliver the material they write, so sometimes the writer envies the comedian. I always liked my writers."

Although Bob has had as many as thirteen writers at one time, he has proven that he is a good ad-libber too.

However, despite being passed over by Oscar and Emmy for direct awards, over the years Bob Hope has received over two thousand honors, awards and citations, including fifty-

four doctorates, that have literally poured in, as well as count-less humanitarian and professional accolades. In 1963, President John Kennedy awarded him a Gold Medal of Honor specially commissioned by Congress—a recognition previously given only to patriotic songwriters George M. Cohan ("Over There," "You're a Grand old Flag," "Yankee Doodle Dandy."), and Irving Berlin ("God Bless America," "Oh, How I Hate to Get Up in the Morning," "Any Bonds Today?")

In 1986, President Ronald Reagan honored Bob at the Kennedy Center for the Performing Arts in Washington.

Selected as "Citizen of the Century" in 1987 during Hollywood's 100th anniversary honoring the USO (United Service Organization) canteens, and presented to him by his friend Jimmy Stewart. And, in 1992, Bob was recognized for his combat zone bravery, receiving the "Life On the Line" award from the General Curtis E. Le May Foundation.

"I got the USO Award the year I didn't leave the country, the year I didn't make a picture I got the Oscar for being a humanitarian, and the B'nai B'rith gave me an award for being a Christian—I can hardly wait to break a leg...It might mean the Nobel Prize."

Speaking of awards, when actor Charlton Heston was con-gratulated for receiving the Kennedy Center award in 1997, he reacted later with these remarks:

"Winning such is indeed a signal honor, for which I'm most grateful, though it does occur to me that the only prize we can be sure we deserve is winning the 50 yard dash in grammar school. All the other accolades, including the Nobel, are subjective. As Ecclesiastics has it....'and it came to me, under the sun, that the race is not always to the swift, nor the battle to the strong, but Time and Chance happeneth to all men.'

"Let's hear it for Time and Chance."

According to Charlton Heston, Bob Hope was presented with the Screen Actor's Guild's First annual Screen Actor's Guild Award for outstanding achievement in fostering the finest ideals of the acting profession. The Academy of Motion Picture Arts and Sciences have honored Bob for his "Unselfish services to the motion picture industry," a life membership in the Academy, and an Oscar for "his contribution to the laughter of the world," and "having hosted the television presentation of the Academy Awards for 14 seasons."

Bob Hope emceed his first Academy Award show in 1941, saying," I'm very happy to be here for my annual insult."

In 1953 he said, "I like to be here in case one of these years they'll have one left over."

1967's opening was: "I don't mind losing, but I hate to go home and explain to my kids how the actors I've been sneering at all year beat me out."

In 1968: "Welcome to the Academy Awards—or, as it's known at my house—*Passover.*"

Bob's opening monologue during the 1978 Oscar presentations ceremony held at the famed Dorothy Chandler Pavilion in Los Angeles, opened with:

"Hey, can you believe this bunch? All on this stage at the same time...it looks like the clearance sale at the Hollywood Wax Museum...nine Oscar winners, right here. I'm the only one who has to show my American Express card to get on the stage...anyway, good evening and welcome to the real 'Star Wars.'"

On stage was, among others, Fred Astaire, Jack Nicholson, Natalie Wood, Kirk Douglas, Greer Garson, Joan Fontaine, Barbara Stanwyck and William Holden.

Having emceed the Academy Awards fourteen times, with other emcee's taking turns, Bob prevails having been host more than anyone else. "And, I wanna tell ya', I loved every minute, no kidding."

Bob's favorite award was as being declared an "Honorary Veteran" in October 1997, alluding to his endless time spent with American servicemen. It is the first and only such award presented by Congress.

Backstage at the twenty-fifth Academy Awards presentations (1953). Cecil B. DeMille, Gloria Swanson, Mary Pickford and Laurence Olivier. *(courtesy Academy of Motion Pictures Arts and Sciences)*

With Dodgers baseball greats.
Tommy Davis, Sandy Koufax and
Don Drysdale *(NBC photo)*

With Shirley Jones
(NBC photo)

★★★★★★★★★★★★★★★★★★★★★★★★★★★★★★★★★★

ACT ELEVEN:
IN THE ARENA

WITH ZEALOUS CRITICS

Catnaps always, anywhere. *(courtesy Paramount Pictures)*

irin: "Why do you do so many benefits, Bob?"
)e: "If you don't, they ask you for money."

onsummate entertainer, Bob Hope is undeniably
s most beloved personality. Hope's rapid chatter
gues are legendary. It's the core of his success. As we
rlier, more people know Bob Hope than any other enter-
in the world. You may ask someone under twenty years
Who is Al Jolson? Clark Gable? Humphrey Bogart? or
even Jack Benny? Chances are they will not know. But they
will certainly be familiar with the name of Bob Hope. Bob
planned it that way, he worked for it, and it worked for him,
although it may have personally cost him in terms of being
generally unavailable to his wife and family, sometimes for
long periods, although Dolores and the kids occasionally traveled with him and appeared on dozens of his shows stateside
and abroad including an appearance at the White House, and
were together on many family vacations.

One of the cornerstones of Bob Hope's personality is that
it is genuine. Other performers act out being outgoing, but in
reality, they suffer and therefore hide behind closed doors, so
to speak. Bob cheerfully loves meeting people without
entourage or armed guards. He drives himself around while at
home. At airports he turns up and waits with all the other pas-
sengers. He goes anywhere he chooses, signs autographs, and
will sit in regular seats without demanding preferential treatment. It is motion—being always on the go—that keeps Bob
Hope young.

How do you become America's most famous citizen? How
does a man like Bob Hope, a master of his art enduring over
75 years with the power to define himself against the ravages
of time and change through his great artistic style, do it?

You work very hard for many years, perhaps a hundred
times harder than anyone else on the planet, more than any
counterpart, and do it consistently for over sixty years. You
appear at hundreds of benefits. Sometimes two in one night.
You author a handful of books, a daily newspaper column, and
dozens of magazine articles. You stick firmly to your agenda
and you make it work. You also hire a corps of gag writers
(100 over time) to help you along.

An organized Bob Hope, who had visions of his dreams
converted into reality, made it all work.

Were Bob not a tireless performer, one who would never quit or ever retire; or didn't, as an artist, constantly needed to be admired, approved of, and applauded; or didn't fuss over beautiful young women; or didn't need to be recognized, or wasn't totally vain, he just wouldn't be Bob Hope and would have hung up his egomaniacal gloves long ago and you would tune into some other show or watch somebody else's late show movies.

Then where would we be? Try to think about entertainment in America without him.

Bob Hope could never resist the temptation to entertain his *guys* and *gals*, the soldiers, sailors, marines and airmen of America's armed forces, even though he had already performed for their fathers, (and some grandfathers during World War II,) making six major trips entertaining not just at the big camps, but at hospital bedsides, from the back of trucks, or at lonely outposts. It made little difference to Bob, who truly loves his work, and the results it brings him what he needs the most—*applause, applause, applause.*

During a lengthily 1984 interview, when Bob and I first met, he rarely looked directly at me, rather, he kept smoothing his hair and checking his tie in a mirror behind me, and rearranged the handkerchief tucked in his front jacket pocket a dozen times, trying to set it right, yet graciously permitting any and all questions, and replying perfectly, clearly, wanting you to know. You felt you knew him, and you did. He allowed you to!

You would have thought he was an entertainer on the way up instead of a global icon well beyond the years of retirement. Eighty-one at that moment, and preparing for a performance onstage within a few minutes, Bob was very much aware of his presence before an interviewer, all the while realizing the camera was catching him in its possessive eye. Bob was constantly posing, a virtual, but involuntary slave to that camera, knowing exactly how to manage himself before it. To Bob, the world revolved around him.

Never cynical, always forgiving, always cheerful, Bob goes on and on despite unfounded criticism. Who are these critics? Why would any reader be interested in unfounded, negative comments concerning the private lives of the great and near great delivered by tabloid hacks? After all, isn't it the man in the arena that really counts, not the critic? It may be that critics' own lives lack something vital, or perhaps it may be simple jealousy? Or maybe uncovering idle gossip about the rich and famous is the reason.

Over the years Bob Hope worked hard, took all the risks, and waged a constant battle within himself to become a major star at almost any cost (except to willfully hurt anyone).

Years ago, when Bob was playing in The Cat and the Canary, fellow actor John Beal recalled this about Bob: *"Nobody gives Bob credit for his discipline and precision of his style. It was a pleasure to play with Bob because he was always on top of things, and moreover, always there for his fellow actors. I kept hearing stories of his upstaging people and always trying to hog the action, but I never found him that way. He actually inspires people who are acting with him in his scenes to give their best—and when they did, he saw to it that they got their minute or more in the sun."*

While in their infancy, Bob experimented in both radio and television at a time when others were fearful or skeptical, and conquered both mediums. When success eluded him as a dancer and singer, Bob experimented with comedy, finally settling for his own brand of standup. Some of his many writers actually complained when he called upon them in the middle of the night to re-work a comedy routine. But, where would they, and he, be without that effort, however gruelling or unconventional. Bob Hope was not a nine-to-five comedian. Some of his writers may have been. Many other entertainers were. Bob always maintained that self promotion was as important as his performances and worked at it his entire career.

Some critics have openly complained about Bob engaging very young and nubile female stars on his shows like Brooke Shields, Loni Anderson, and others allowing the girls to kiss him, stating "...that's something that just doesn't happen to people who are in their eighties." Bob Hope has never grown up in his craft, maintaining a youthful spirit even to that effect. Even at 90, Bob continually enjoyed the company of pretty young women. More jealousy, I suspect, from the pen of critics overlooking the arena from the far-flung bleachers.

Jealousy obviously plays a weighty part. Over the years, criticism of Bob's topical humor or barbs directed towards personalities like his friend, Bing Crosby, as well as Presidents and other icons, persisted throughout his career. But, why?

Comedian Don Rickles built an entire career disrespecting everyone, emitting considerably worse material than Bob could ever dream of. No one criticizes Rickles, because that's his style of entertaining, and it is accepted.

I remember singer Jerry Vale telling me how worried he used to be when Don Rickles, as a young comedian, would say outrageous things directed at patrons in his audience, and Don subsequently explained, laughingly, "When we worked on shows together many years ago, Jerry was a nervous wreck because I made fun of people as part of my act. It almost put him in a rest home. It's my style of comedy! He would say that people were walking out on me. Calm down, Jerry, I told him, it's only comedy- not real life. Jerry, still a good friend, was concerned for me, but he didn't have to be."

And, as Jerry Vale observed: "But Bob Hope, because he is so much larger than life, and therefore observed more carefully and criticized more frequently, is singled out by ambitious pundits who may be jealous of his tremendous and enduring success, or perhaps they find him an easy target just as Bob found it equally comfortable to poke fun at anyone and everyone including presidents, kings and queens, politicians, musicians, and anyone else in his sights, notwithstanding. But those barbs were kindly, even loving, and certainly, not vicious."

During those ubiquitous USO tours Bob always took his role as a patriot quite seriously. A review of the tapes of those available shows demonstrates the appreciation found deep in the eyes and smiles—always smiles—of servicemen he visited regularly to entertain everywhere from Europe to the Pacific during World War II right through the Korean and Vietnam wars, and even beyond. When you hear the serious tribute he delivers at the close of each television special, you will understand the true agenda of Bob Hope.

Listen and appreciate.

Early in 2001, when Mel Brooks presented the very successful Broadway musical play *The Producers*, he evoked the following valid comment that might apply to Bob Hope:

> *"If you're serious about show business, remember the loudest noise gets the best attention, so don't tiptoe into show business....jump into show business."*

Bob stomped into show business!

Early on some people considered him to be a cheap vaude-ville comic who loved only himself. However, like Frank Sinatra, Bob has also quietly contributed largely to more charities than anyone will ever know. He provides countless personal favors for many, involving much money and time, and has never complained or spoke publicly about them. His reputation as a Jack Benny style cheapskate was unfairly documented by people who assembled around him for anything they could get, but were rebuffed. After many years Bob and Dolores finally placed a stop (or limit) to that drain.

More recently, a hack writer, at best, apparently trained in Senator Joseph McCarthy's 1950s accusing style (literally citing vital, damning information from unnamed sources aimed against a selected subject) wrote negatively about Bob in a book that I consider blasphemous, indefensible and totally irreverent; a coward's comments published when Bob was at an advanced age and unable to effectively respond. That writer wasn't brave enough to have published that memoir of Bob Hope when Bob could have responded and ripped him apart with his very effective barbs. Those petty complaints, mostly unsupported, were dismal sounding, indeed! That writer had stupendous nerve publicly invading the personal privacy of Bob and his family, spreading negative comments from embittered family members and those close to Bob Hope in the person of servants, security people, writers, etc., all which bear little relevance to Bob's great career.

What was accomplished? Why did they try to tear down the reputation of a wonderful entertainer who has brought priceless cheer and good will to millions? To what end? For who's benefit? Perhaps it was an editor's sure-fire method to promote and sell tabloid-style books and magazines for his publisher.

Well, it did not work. Bob's excellent reputation remains effectively valid and intact.

Soon, you will be able to track Bob's life in comedy during one visit to his Museum of Comedy, now in the planning stage.

★★★★★★★★★★★★★★★★★★★★★★★★★★★★★★★

ACT TWELVE:
HOPE'S HUMOR

SAMPLES FROM THE VAULT

"Now, where was I?" *(courtesy NBC)*

Groucho Marx considered Bob Hope a translator, taking writers and others jokes and delivering them relying on the joke itself and his own likable personality to win over an audience. He makes fun of everyone associated with an audience, including the President of the United States. So, no one gets mad. If he is successful roasting Presidents, how can anyone resent his gags.

HOPE: Well, it's Groucho Marx.
(applause)
GROUCHO: You call that an introduction? The doctor got more applause when he took out my appendix.
HOPE: Why are you so upset? I want you to feel at home. I want you to feel that you belong here.
GROUCHO: As if I belong here? Hope, I know when I've been insulted. I'm leaving here immediately.
HOPE: Just a minute, Groucho....we've been friends a long time. I don't want you to leave hating me.
GROUCHO: Why not, that's the way I came in.

*****

SAN FRANCISCO: When you lay an egg here it rolls down the hill and disappears into the bay.

*****

WEATHER; Gee, if this snow gets any deeper, I'll have to put a shorter string on my Yo-Yo.

*****

COAST GUARD: This is Bob "Coast Guard" Hope, telling you to put Pepsodent on your brush and use plenty of traction and none of your teeth will be missing in action. Yes, the Coast Guard—I wanna tell ya...these are the boys who guard the coast and they really guard it well. The only problem they have here today is finding it. We've had some over ambitious dew falling around here the last few days. The Chamber of Commerce wouldn't admit it was raining so hard until this morning....when the USS Arkansas anchored at Sunset and Vine.

*****

MARINES: You know what a Marine is...that's a booby trap that's on our side. During the time they stay in boot camp these Marines have to forget completely about girls. In fact, at midnight the sergeant goes through the barracks with a flashlight waking up anybody who has a smile on his face.

*****

BOB: You're a small girl, Ida. You hardly come up to my chin.
IDA: Which one?
BOB: Those aren't chins. That's a staircase for my Adams Apple.

*****

NEW YORK: I was surprised to see so many homeless people on the streets. The first one I met was Mayor Ed Koch. He finally found out what it felt like to be mugged.

BROADWAY: I can't believe the ticket prices. When I was doing *Roberta* on Broadway, if you paid that kind of money, you owned a piece of the show...*and* the leading lady. I heard a mugger tell a tourist, *"Your Phantom of the Opera tickets, or your life."*

*****

My name is Colonel Robert Hope. I've had a brilliant career...twenty years in the Air Force...but only two hours in the air. I wouldn't have had those, but one day I got hit by a Jeep.

The plane I chartered to fly here was really a clunk. It had canvas wings that flapped. But the guy only charged me fifty dollars. That included the pilot, a small can of propeller oil, and prayer books for everybody.

We were flying at just the right altitude. Any higher, my nose would start to bleed. Any lower, the bomb bay would scoop up cocker spaniels.

Jane: Stop worrying about a plane crashing, Bob. Look at Les Brown's musicians back there—look how relaxed they are!

Bob: Yes, but they were in that condition when we carried them on the plane.

USO TOURS

Boy, GI audiences are wonderful. They never walk out on you. Those M.P.s made wonderful ushers.

Look at this kid ogle Marilyn Maxwell. First time I ever saw two eyeballs turn into bomb sights.

England is a great place for a comedian to work. It's an island, so the audience can't run very far.

*****

Vera Vague: Gee Bob, where did you learn to kiss like that?
Bob: I used to blow up balloons for a weather station.

*****

Bob Hope was the last speaker during a Friars Club dinner held for Jack Benny:

"Last time Jack paid one hundred dollars a plate, it was to his dentist....I don't know how old Jack really is, but a couple of years ago he went to Rome, saw the Colosseum, and said, 'It's nice, if you like modern.'"

★★★★★★★★★★★★★★★★★★★★★★★★★★★★★★★★

ACT THIRTEEN:
SUMMING UP

WARD GRANT'S OWN WORDS

Bob and Dolores meet again *(courtesy NBC photos)*

WARD GRANT'S OWN WORDS

"I think in the course of his lifetime the man and his image have blended together, so you cannot separate the man and his image; the images that the people see is basically the man himself."

Ward Grant: from Portrait of a Superstar, by Charles Thompson, 1981

★★★★★★★★★★★★★★★★★★★★★★★★★★★★★★

ACT FOURTEEN:
ACKNOWLEDGMENTS

THANKING EVERYONE

....
"Thanks for the Memory, Bob!" 1986 Westbury, N.Y. *(C. Camille Smith photo)*
....

GIVING THANKS

I wish to acknowledge the many contributors who unselfishly joined with me to produce this tribute to Bob Hope. First, *Les Girls*: Jane Russell, Connie Haines, Rhonda Fleming, and Beryl Davis, all enthusiastically encouraging me all through the process; Jane with her very original foreword of *love*, Connie, always cheerful, full of ideas and advice, encouraging the book from its inception. Beryl Davis with the same kind of enthusiasm, and Rhonda Fleming, Bob's co-star and part of the beautiful quartet of Hope admirers. This stalwart group, still friends today, once toured together as a singing act performing Bible songs for millions- assisted by their friend Bob Hope- whose energy was contagious and right on the mark.

Thanks goes to Ward Grant, Bob's longtime Press Agent, for his assistance from Bob's California office; author, actress, Broadway star Kathryn Crosby, who always cares and helps; my pal of twenty years, Patty Andrews of the Andrews Sisters, for her usual good-natured enthusiasm; Charlton Heston, with always a noble and definitive word; Frankie Laine, my original mentor; longtime buddies Ann Jillian and her husband/manager Andy Murcia; Broadcaster Al Monroe, who sends material and recommends ideas, including mentions in his Society of Singer's, New York column and on his New Jersey radio show; the enduring Jerry Vale, a really grounded friend who suggested and supplied the whereabouts of some Hope contributors, and for enlightening words; Joe Pardee, my human music library, generously supplying recordings and song title whereabouts; Ben Grisafi, musical advisor, prolific arranger and conductor of his own Big Band; Jerry Castleman, a working associate full of good ideas; "Singing Santa's" leader Brooke Bonomi who supplied great information and photos; Cori Britt and Doc Giffen of Arnold Palmer's office; Scott Tolley of (Jack) Nicklaus Communications; musical director Lee Hale, fellow scribe, with always an encouraging word; the USO Organization in Washington who furnished venue lists and photos; Nadia Pollard of NBC, New York for assistance in obtaining permission to feature their great photos; my neglected wife, Jeanette; my son Bob for talking me into this hardworking I-Mac and instructing me in its use without pain; and, of course, the great and wonderful Bob and Dolores Hope.

Special Credits

Thanks for the Memory from the Paramount Picture
BIG BROADCAST OF 1938
Words and Music by Leo Robin and Ralph Rainger
Copyright © 1948 (Renewed 1975) by Famous Music Corporation
International Copyright Secured. All rights reserved.

Buttons And Bows
from the Paramount Motion picture PALEFACE
Words and Music by Jay Livingston and Ray Evans
Copyright © 1948 (Renewed 1975) by Famous Music Corporation
International Copyright secured. All rights reserved.

Two Sleepy People
from the Paramount Motion Picture THANKS FOR THE MEMORY
Words by Frank Loesser
Music by Hoagy Carmichael
Copyright © 1938 (Renewed1965) by Famous Music Corporation
International Copyright secured. All rights reserved.

Special thanks to Lissa Wales, unique photographer of drummers, for
her exclusive photo of Bob Hope and Jack Nicklaus on page 57.
(Lissaw@juno.com - www.drumpics.com)

Remembering C. Camille Smith for his photos of Bob Hope with
Richard Grudens, and Ann Jillian.

Ben Grisafi
(left) and Jerry
Castleman

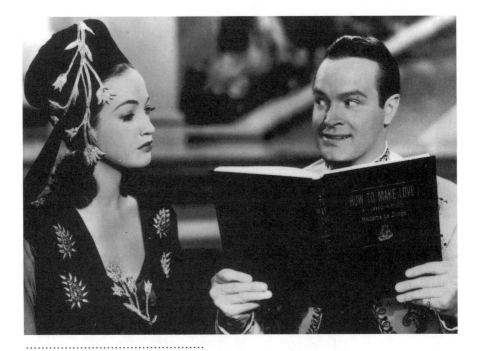

Bob and Hedy Lamarr in "My Favorite Spy"
(courtesy Paramount Pictures)

★★★★★★★★★★★★★★★★★★★★★★★★★★★★★★★

ACT FIFTEEN:
THE LISTS

BROADWAY - MOVIES - USO TOURS

The Palace Theater, N.Y. Circa, 1921
(N.Y. Historical Society)

ALL THOSE TALKING MOVIES

1. FEBRUARY 18, 1938, *THE BIG BROADCAST* OF 1938-Bob's absolute film debut except for a few shorts. His hit song and longtime theme "Thanks for the Memory" won an Academy Award. With Dorothy Lamour, Martha Raye, W.C. Fields, Ben Blue and Shirley Ross

2. APRIL 29, 1938, *COLLEGE SWING* with George Burns and Gracie Allen, Betty Grable, & Martha Raye.

3. AUGUST 19, 1938, *GIVE ME A SAILOR* with Martha Raye, Betty Grable and Jack Whiting.

4. NOVEMBER 11, 1938, *THANKS FOR THE MEMORY* with Shirley Ross and Charles Butterworth and Hope introduced another standard "Two Sleepy People."

5. APRIL 14, 1939, *NEVER DAY DIE* with Martha Raye, Andy Devine and Alan Mowbray.

6. MAY 19, 1939, *SOME LIKE IT HOT* with Shirley Ross, Una Merkel, and Gene Krupa. (Not the one with Marilyn and Jack Lemmon.)

7. NOVEMBER 10, 1939, *THE CAT AND THE CANARY* with Paulette Goddard was first planned Hope vehicle and established him as a strong crowd pleaser.

8. MARCH 22, 1940, *ROAD TO SINGAPORE* The first of the road films and an immediate smash with Bing Crosby and Dorothy Lamour, combined to perfection. Also with Jerry Colonna and Anthony Quinn.

9. JUNE 21, 1940, *THE GHOST BREAKERS* with Paulette Goddard, Paul Lukas, Richard Carlson, and Anthony Quinn.

10. APRIL 11, 1941, *ROAD TO ZANZIBAR* with Bing, Dorothy, and Una Merkel with "You Lucky People, You" as top tune.

11. JULY 4, 1941, *CAUGHT IN THE DRAFT* with Dorothy Lamour, Eddie Bracken and Lynne Overman, where he ends up a hero, after all.

12. OCTOBER 10, 1941, *NOTHING BUT THE TRUTH* with Paulette Goddard, Edward Arnold and Leif Erikson.

13. DECEMBER 25, 1941, *LOUISIANA PURCHASE* was adapted from it's Broadway sister with Hope, Victor Moore and Vera Zorina

14. MARCH 18, 1942, *MY FAVORITE BLONDE* Bob with Madeline Carroll and George Zucco

15. October 5, 1942, *ROAD TO MOROCCO*, another road show with Bing and Dorothy with the song "Moonlight Becomes You" and help from Anthony Quinn and Donna Drake.

16. DECEMBER 31, 1942, *STAR SPANGLED RHYTHM*, This all-star vehicle starred everyone who was under contract on the Paramount lot including Betty Hutton, Bing Crosby, Alan Ladd, Dick Powell, Mary Martin, Susan Hayward and others.

17. JANUARY 4, 1943, (RKO RADIO) *THEY GOT ME COVERED* with Dorothy Lamour, Otto Preminger, & Donald Meek (Remember him?).

18. AUGUST 5, 1943, *LET'S FACE IT*. Again with Betty Hutton, Zasu Pitts, & Joe Sawyer.

19. OCTOBER 17, 1944, *THE PRINCESS AND THE PIRATE* (RKO RADIO) With Virginia Mayo, Walter Brennan, Victor McLaglen, and Walter Slezak.

20. SEPTEMBER, 1945, *ROAD TO UTOPIA*, with Bing and Dorothy, Hillary Brooke and Robert Benchley. Another very funny "Road" film.

My Favorite Spy, 1951 *(courtesy Paramount Pictures)*

21. S E P T E M B E R 30, 1946, *MON-SIEUR BEAU-CAIRE*, an Errol Flynn-like movie for Bob with Joan Caulfield and Marjorie Reynolds.

22. APRIL 4, 1947, *MY FAVORITE BRUNETTE* with Hope Enterprises running things starred Bob with Dorothy Lamour and a guest spot with Bing. Also starring heavies Lon Chaney, and Peter Lorre.

23. AUGUST 29, 1947, *VARIETY GIRL* off the road with Bing, Olga San Juan and more contract players at Paramount including a Bob Hope vignette with Bing.

24. NOVEMBER 21, 1947, *WHERE THERE'S LIFE* with William Bendix, Signe Hasso, and George Coulouris.

25. DECEMBER 25, 1947, *ROAD TO RIO*, the fifth "Road" show with Dorothy and Bing and the song "But Beautiful," also with "Professor" Jerry Colonna.

26. DECEMBER 24, 1948, *THE PALEFACE* with lovely Jane Russell, Bob's lifelong friend who wrote this book's foreword.

27. JULY 4, 1949, *SORROWFUL JONES* with Lucille ("I Love Lucy") Ball, Bruce Cabot and Thomas Gomez.

28. DECEMBER 28, 1949, *THE GREAT LOVER* with Rhonda Fleming, Roland Young, and George Reeves.

29. JULY 19, 1950, *FANCY PANTS* with Lucille Ball again, Bruce Cabot and Jack Kirkwood.

30. MARCH 8, 1951, *THE LEMON DROP KID* with Marilyn Maxwell and Lloyd Nolan.

31. December 27, 1951, *MY FAVORITE SPY* with Hedy Lamarr, Francis L. Sullivan and Mike Mazurki.

32. JULY 14, 1952, *SON OF PALEFACE* with that Russell gal again who literally ties everyone up, including Roy Rogers, Iron Eye Cody, and Bill Williams.

33. NOVEMBER 19, 1952, *ROAD TO BALI* with that happy gang: Crosby, Hope, and Lamour on another trip-Katherine Hepburn and Humphrey Bogart pull the African Queen across the screen in a cameo, too. The Crosby—Hope tune is "Chicago Style."

34. FEBRUARY 19, 1953, *OFF LIMITS*, this time with Mickey Rooney, Marilyn Maxwell and Jack Dempsey.

35. OCTOBER 22, 1953, *HERE COME THE GIRLS* who are Arlene Dahl and Rosemary Clooney, backed by Tony Martin of "Casbah" fame, and the Four Step Brothers.

36. MARCH 1, 1954, *CASANOVA'S BIG NIGHT* with Joan Fontaine, John Carridine, Basil (Sherlock Holmes) Rathbone, and Lon (Frankenstein) Chaney.

37. MAY 31, 1955, *THE SEVEN LITTLE FOYS* with James Cagney and Bob doing some great dance sequences, with George Tobias, Milly Vitale and Angela Clarke.

38. JUNE 4, 1956, *THAT CERTAIN FEELING* with Eva Marie Saint, George Sanders, Pearl Bailey and Al Capp (Lil Abner's creator). Great songs: "That Certain Feeling" and "Zing! Went the Strings of My Heart."

39. DECEMBER 21, 1956, (Produced in England by MGM) *THE IRON PETTICOAT* also starring Katherine Hepburn, Robert Helpmann, and David Kossoff.

40. JUNE 7, 1957, *BEAU JAMES* with Vera Miles, Paul Douglas, and George Jessel, Bob's old vaudeville buddy.

41. MARCH 7, 1958, *PARIS HOLIDAY* (United Artists) with Anita Ekberg, Martha Hyer, Preston Sturges, and the great comedian Fernandel.

42. MARCH 20, 1959, *ALIAS JESSE JAMES* (United Artists) set Bob with Rhonda Fleming once again as well as Wendell Corey and Jim Davis.

43. NOVEMBER 14, 1960, *THE FACTS OF LIFE* (United Artists) with Lucille Ball, Ruth Hussey, Louis Nye and Mike Mazurki.

44. NOVEMBER 16, 1961, *BACHELOR IN PARADISE* (MGM) with Lana Turner, Janis Paige, Jim Hunter, and Agnes Moorehead.

45. MAY 22, 1962, *ROAD TO HONG KONG* (United Artists-England) with the weary trio, Joan Collins, and Robert Morley.The last "Road" movie.

46. APRIL 1, 1963, *CRITIC'S CHOICE* (Warner Bros.) employs Lucille Ball, Marilyn Maxwell, & Jim (voice of Mr. Magoo) Backus.

47. JUNE 14, 1963, *CALL ME BWANA* (United Artists-England) with Anita Ekberg, Edie Adams, and Arnold Palmer, Bob's golfing buddy.

48. JANUARY 30, 1964, *A GLOBAL AFFAIR* (MGM) and Yvonne De Carlo, Robert Sterling, and Lilo Pulver.

49. JUNE 2, 1965, *I'LL TAKE SWEDEN* (United Artists) with Tuesday Weld, Frankie Avalon, Dina Merrill, and Jeremy Slate.

50. JUNE 1, 1966, *BOY, DID I GET A WRONG NUMBER* (United Artists) with Elke Sommer, Phyllis Diller, and Harry Von Zell (Eddie Cantor's radio show announcer-Remember?).

51. APRIL 4, 1967, *EIGHT ON THE LAM* (United Artists) with Diller, Jonathon Winters, Jill St. John, and some of

the Hope family including grandkids Avis Hope and Robert Hope.

52. MAY 8, 1968, *THE PRIVATE NAVY OF SGT. O'FARRELL* (United Artists) with Diller once again, Gina Lollobrigida, and Jeffrey Hunter.

53. MAY 28, 1971, *HOW TO COMMIT MARRIAGE* (Cinerama) with Jackie Gleason, Jane (the first Mrs. Reagan) Wyman, Leslie Nielsen, Tina Louise and Irwin Corey.

54. OCTOBER 15, 1972, *CANCEL MY RESERVATION* (Warner Bros.) with Eva Marie Saint, Ralph Bellamy, Forrest Tucker and Keenan Wynn.

THE SHORTS:

Going Spanish, 1934 Educational Films,
Paree, Paree, 1934 Warner Brothers
The Old Gray Mayor, 1935 Warner Brothers
Watch the Birdie, 1935 Warner Brothers
Double Exposure, 1935 Warner Brothers
Calling All Tars, 1936 Warner Brothers
Shop Talk, 1936 Warner Brothers

And a handful of golf, wartime bond selling, and Variety Clubs shorts, as well.

Don't Hook Now, 1938 (Golf)
Welcome to Britain. 1943 (Orientation film for the military)
All-Star Bond Rally. 1945 (selling war bonds)
Hollywood Victory Caravan. 1945. (selling war bonds)
The Heart of Show Business. 1957 (for the Variety Clubs)
Showdown at Ulcer Gulch. 1958 (promo for magazine)
Hollywood Star-Spangled Revue. (selling Treasury bonds)

Bob also appeared briefly in "The Greatest Show on Earth" in 1952 in a cameo; "Scared Stiff" in 1953 as a guest in the Martin & Lewis film; in "The Five Pennies" 1959, as himself in a cameo; and finally in "The Oscar", a cameo as himself as an Oscar emcee.

That's All Folks!

The Broadway Shows: Bob Hope Played Here

1927 *SIDEWALKS OF NEW YORK*, with Ruby Keeler. "Al Jolson, her husband, used to pick her up at the theater every night after the show."

1932 *BALLYHOO OF 1932* with Lulu McConnell, Willie Howard and Grace Hartman. First opened in Atlantic City.

1933 *ROBERTA*, by Jerome Kern and Otto Harbach with (later, Senator) George Murphy, Fay Tempelton, Tamara, Ray Middleton, Sydney Greenstreet, Fred McMurray. Song: "Smoke Gets In Your Eyes."
1934 *SAY WHEN*, with Harry Richman, Prince Mike Romanoff, and Linda Watkins.

1936 *ZIEGFELD FOLLIES*, Wintergarden Theater, by Vernon Duke and Ira Gershwin, with Fannie Brice, Eve Arden, Gertrude Niesen, Judy Canova, Song: "I Can't Get Started."

1936 *RED HOT & BLUE*, Cole Porter, with Jimmy Durante, Ethel Merman, Vivian Vance. Hit Song: "It's De -Lovely."

The USO Tours
Dangerous Vacation Spots

Alaska, 1942; USS Shangri-la, Bay of Naples 1963; Bizerte, North Africa, 1943; Tunis, North Africa 1943;

Diyarbakir, Turkey, 1963; Marrakech, Tunis, 1943; Palermo, Sicily, 1943; Subic Bay, Philippines, 1964; Polebrook, AFB, England 1943; Tan Son Nhut, Vietnam, 1964; Tarawa, South Pacific, 1943; Da Nang, Vietnam, 1965, 68, 69; Algiers, North Africa, 1943; Dominican Republic, 1965; Guadalcanal, South Pacific, 1944; USS Ticonderoga, China Sea, 1965; Brisbane & Sydney, Australia, 1945; Qui Nhon, Vietnam, 1966; Amiens & Chateau, France, 1945; Chu Lai, Vietnam, 1966; Marseilles, France 1945; Guam, South Pacific, 1967; Munich & Nuremberg, Germany 1958; USS Ranger, China Sea, 1967; Wiesbaden, Germany 1948; Sanctuary (Hospital Ship), Azores, 1958; China Sea, 1967; Berlin, Germany, 1948; USS New Jersey, Vietnam, 1968; Anchorage, Alaska, 1949; Okinawa, South Pacific, 1968; Seoul, Korea, 1950 & 1953; Incirli, Turkey, 1969; Tokyo, Japan, 1950; Souda Bay, Crete, 1970; Tripler Army Hospital, Hawaii, 1950; Osan AFB, Korea, 1970; Goose Bay, Labrador, 1954; Hanau, Germany, 1970; Panama Canal Zone, 1960; USS John Kennedy, Crete, 1970; Antiqua, West Indies, 1960; Rota, Spain, 1971; Guantanamo Bay, Cuba, 1960 & 1971; Wake Island, 1972; Argentina, 1961; USS Midway, Singapore, 1972; Clark Field, Philippines, 1962; Yakota, Japan, 1972; Panmunjom, Korea, 1962; Namphong, Thailand, 1972; Formosa, 1962; Diego Garcia, Indian Ocean, 1972; USS Okinawa, Persian Gulf, 1988

On the USS Shangri-La, Bay of
Naples, 1963. *(US Navy photo)*

BIBLIOGRAPHY

Barthel, Joan. *Bob Hope*. Life Magazine, January 1971

Bennett, Tony, with Will Friedwald, *The Good Life*, New York, New York: Simon E. Schuster, 1998.

Crosby, Bing, with Pete Martin. *Call Me Lucky*. New York, New York: Simon and Shuster, 1953

Crosby, Kathryn, *Bing and Other Things*, New York, New York: Meredith Press, 1967

Day, Doris, with A.E. Hotchner. *Doris Day-Her Own Story*. New York, New York: William Morrow, 1975

Faith, William Robert. *Bob Hope—A Life In Comedy*. New York, New York: G.P. Putnam's Sons, 1982

Fein, Irving A., *Jack Benny-An Intimate Biography*, New York, New York: G.P. Putnam's Sons, 1976

Grudens, Richard, *The Music Men*. Stonybrook, New York: Celebrity Profiles Publishing, 1998

Grudens, Richard, *Bob Hope-The Show Goes On*, *World War II* Magazine, September, 1995

Grudens, Richard, *Reliving Bob Hope's USO Tours*, California Highway Patrolman Magazine, August 1989

Grudens, Richard, *Thanks for the Memories* Volkswagen's World Magazine, Spring 1986

Harris, Jay, Editor, by Neil Hickey. *The Comedian Turns Serious*, TV Guide -The First 25 Years. New York: Simon and Schuster, 1978

Hope, Bob, *This Is On Me*. London, England: Frederick Muller Ltd., 1954 No Copyright listed.

O'Connell, Sheldon, with Gord Atkinson, *Bing-A Voice for All Seasons*. Republic of Ireland: Kerryman, Ltd., 1984

Russell, Jane, *Jane Russell-My Paths & Detours*. Thorndike, Maine: Thorndike Press, 1985

Sforza, John, *Swing It-The Andrews Sisters Story*, Lexington, Kentucky: University Press of Kentucky, 2000.

Thompson, Charles, *Bob Hope—Portrait of a Superstar*. New York, New York: St. Martin's Press, 1981

Watson, Thomas, J. and Bill Chapman, *Judy-Portrait of An American Legend*. New York, New York: McGraw-Hill Company 1986

Whiting, Margaret, and Will Holt. *It Might as Well Be Spring*. New York, New York: William Morrow & Company, Inc. 1987

ABOUT THE AUTHOR

Richard Grudens of Stony Brook, New York, was initially influenced by Pulitzer Prize dramatist Robert Anderson; *New York Herald Tribune* columnist Will Cuppy; and detective/mystery writer Dashiell Hammett, all whom he knew in his early years. Grudens worked his way up from a studio page in NBC studios in New York to newswriter for such names as H.V. Kaltenborn, John Cameron Swayze, and Bob & Ray. Feature writing for Long Island P.M. Magazine (1980-86) led to his first book, *The Best Damn Trumpet Player—Memories of the Big Band Era*. He has written over 100 magazine articles on diverse subjects from interviews with legendary cowboy Gene Autry in *Wild West Magazine* in 1995 to a treatise on the Beach Boys in the *California Highway Patrol Magazine*. His exclusive interview with Bob Hope about his USO tours was published in *World War II Magazine*.

His other books include *The Song Stars*—about the girl singers (1997); *The Music Men*—about the men singers (1998); *Jukebox Saturday Night*—more memories of the Big Band Era (1999); *Snootie Little Cutie—The Connie Haines Story*, and *Magic Moments—The Sally Bennett Story* (2000), *Jerry Vale—A Singer's Life* (2001).

Commenting about the book *Jukebox Saturday Night* in 1999, Kathryn (Mrs. Bing) Crosby wrote, "Richard Grudens is the musical historian of our time. Without him, the magic would be lost forever. We all owe him a debt that we can never repay."

Richard Grudens, Jerry and Rita Vale at Border's Book signing, Farmingdale, NY, October 2001

INDEX

Truman, Bess, 137,
Truman, Harry (President), 136, 137,
Trump, Donald, 90,

U

Utley, Garrick, 127,

V

Vague, Vera, 119, 166,
Vale, Jerry, 59, 60, 100, 161, 170, 186,
Vale, Rita, 186,
Vallee, Rudy, 29,
Van Heusen, Jimmy, 71,

W

Wales, Lissa, 171,

Wallace, Henry (Vice President), 120,
Warren, Fran, 98,
Wayne, John, 50, 112,
Welch, Raquel, 112, 127,
West, Mae, 38,
Westmoreland, William (General), 112, 127,
Whiting, Margaret, 32, 98, 112, 120,
Whiting, Richard, 98,
Whiteman, Paul, 67,
Wilder, Patricia (Honey Chile), 30,
Winchell, Walter, 29, 89,
Wood, Natalie, 50, 154,
Wyman, Jane, 130, 132,

CELEBRITY PROFILES PUBLISHING
BOX 344 Main Street
STONY BROOK, NY 11790

(631) 862-8555 • FAX (631) 862-0139 • e-mail: celebpro4@aol.com

The BEST DAMN TRUMPET PLAYER   Copies _____
ISBN 1-57579-011-4   196 Pages   55 Photos
Price $15.95
****

The SONG STARS   Copies _____
ISBN 1-57579-045-9   240 Pages   60 Photos
Price $17.95
****

The MUSIC MEN   Copies _____
ISBN 1-57579-097-1   250 Pages   70 Photos
PRICE $17.95
****

JUKEBOX SATURDAY NIGHT   Copies_____
ISBN 1-57579-142-0   250 Pages   70 Photos
PRICE $17.95
****

SNOOTIE LITTLE CUTIE — The Connie Haines Story   Copies_____
ISBN 1-57579-143-9   144 Pages   77 Photos
PRICE $17.95
****

JERRY VALE — A Singer's Life   Copies_____
ISBN 1-57579-176-5   216 Pages   117 Photos
PRICE $19.95

****

THE SPIRIT OF BOB HOPE —
One Hundred Years, One Million Laughs   Copies_____
ISBN 1-57579-227-3   208 Pages   132 Photos
PRICE $19.95
****

NAME _____

ADDRESS_____

CITY, TOWN, STATE_____ ZIP CODE_____

Include $3.50 for Priority Mail (2 days arrival time) for up to 2 books.
Enclose check or money order. Order will be shipped immediately.

For CREDIT CARDS, please fill out as shown below:

Card #_____ Exp. Date_____

Signature_____

VISA ___AMEX ___ DISCOVER___MASTER CARD___(CHECK ONE)